OREAD INSTITUTE.

THE

CARPENTER'S ASSISTANT:

CONTAINING

A SUCCINCT ACCOUNT

OF

EGYPTIAN, GRECIAN AND ROMAN ARCHITECTURE.

ALSO, A DESCRIPTION OF THE

TUSCAN, DORIC, IONIC, CORINTHIAN AND COMPOSITE ORDERS;

TOGETHER WITH

SPECIFICATIONS, PRACTICAL RULES AND TABLES FOR CARPENTERS, AND A GLOSSARY OF ARCHITECTURAL TERMS.

ILLUSTRATED WITH

NEARLY 200 PLATES OF PLANS, ELEVATIONS, DETAILS, AND PRACTICAL STAIR-BUILDING.

By WILLIAM BROWN, Architect.

REVISED, IMPROVED AND ENLARGED, WITH ADDITIONS

ON

RURAL ARCHITECTURE;

EMBRACING

PLANS, ELEVATIONS, GROUNDS, &c., &c., OF COTTAGES, VILLAS, AND FARM-BUILDINGS.

By LEWIS E. JOY, Architect.

FIFTH EDITION.

WORCESTER:
PUBLISHED BY EDWARD LIVERMORE.
BOSTON: BENJAMIN B. MUSSEY & Co.; PHILLIPS, SAMPSON & Co. PHILADELPHIA: THOMAS, COWPERTHWAITE & Co. NEW YORK: PRATT, WOODFORD & Co; A. S. BARNES & Co. BUFFALO: GEORGE H. DERBY & Co.
1852.

Stereotyped by
HOBART & ROBBINS;
NEW ENGLAND TYPE AND STEREOTYPE FOUNDERY,
BOSTON.

PREFACE.

In preparing this treatise on Architecture, the author has aimed to furnish a work suited to the wants of the carpenter. He has long felt the necessity of such a work, and hoped that some one better qualified than himself would have supplied the deficiency; but, as no one has attempted this task, the author considers it a duty which he owes to his fellow-laborers, to offer them the following treatise.

It is not intended, in this work, to enter minutely into the principles of architecture, for this would extend it to several volumes, and subject those for whom it is mainly designed to unnecessary expense. The author has endeavored, however, to combine, in as brief and concise a manner as possible, all that is absolutely necessary for the student who aims at a practical knowledge of carpentry, and not at finished classical attainments in the study of architecture, either as a science or an art. And he flatters himself that he has done this in a manner so clear and intelligible, that a knowledge of this branch of science may be acquired by the assiduous and careful student, without the assistance of an instructor.

The peculiar advantages of this work are its simplicity, its singular adaptedness to the wants of the carpenter, and its freedom from technicalities, which are so abundant in many treatises of this kind. A few technical words, however, have been admitted, of necessity, because the same idea could not be so well expressed without a tedious circumlocution; but these terms are fully explained in a Glossary which is appended.

In order that the learner may be furnished with some data on which to found his architectural knowledge, who has not the time or the means to examine more extensive works, we have given a short history of the origin of architecture, with a brief account of its three principal styles, namely, Egyptian, Grecian, and Roman; also, a description of the five orders,—

the Tuscan, Doric, Ionic, Corinthian, and Composite. By the aid of this cursory view, he will be enabled to form an idea of the grandeur and magnificence of ancient architecture, and the extent to which a cultivation of the art was carried before the overthrow of the Grecian cities and the downfall of the Roman Empire. He must not, however, deceive himself by supposing that, when he has acquired all the principles contained in this little treatise, he has become master of the whole subject of architecture; for it is one to which the brightest intellect and the most powerful talents might be devoted to a declining old age; and then the individual would exclaim, like the celebrated Newton, "Alas! I have gathered only a few pebbles on the shore of the great ocean of knowledge."

As the student is supposed to have some knowledge of the elements of mathematics, the author has not thought proper to admit anything of this character into the work, with the exception of a few elementary principles of Geometry.

To relieve the carpenter from tedious numerical calculations, several valuable tables are annexed.

It was the design of the author to prepare a treatise adapted expressly to the actual wants of the carpenter, which he, having had many years' experience in practical carpentry, has known and felt; and if he shall have succeeded, in offering the following work, it will not be labor lost, and his object will be obtained.

While preparing this volume, we have been prevented from attending so closely as we could have wished to the revision of our manuscript, and it is possible that a few errors may have crept in from an oversight in the proof. We trust, however, that the book will be found to be as free from inaccuracies as any of its size and character.

WILLIAM BROWN.

Lowell, Mass., 1847.

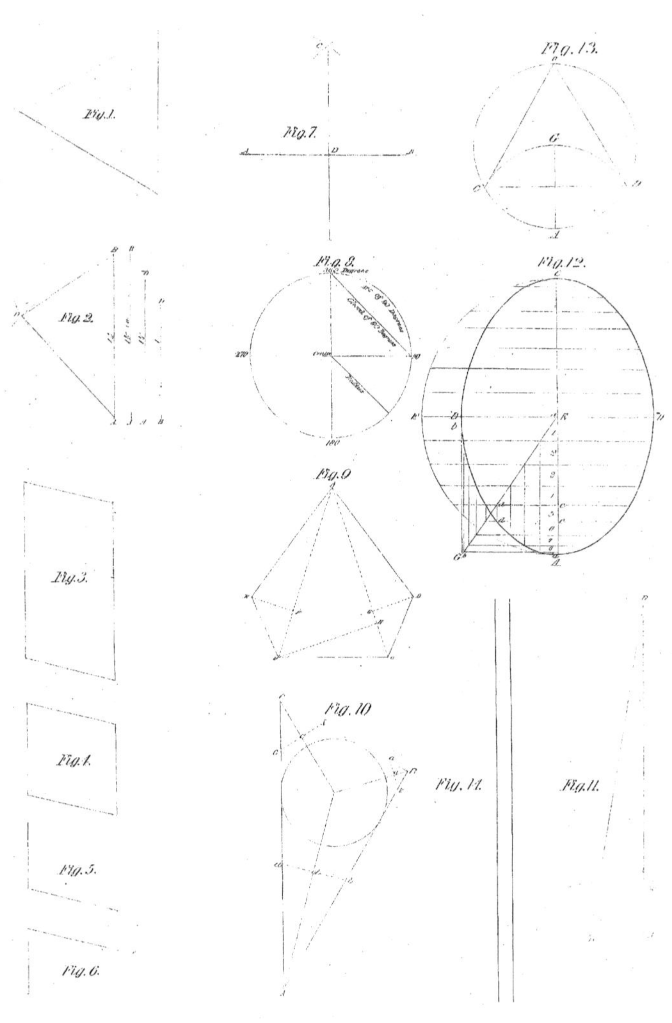
Fig. 1.
Fig. 7.
Fig. 13.
Fig. 2.
Fig. 8.
Fig. 12.
Fig. 3.
Fig. 9
Fig. 4.
Fig. 10
Fig. 14.
Fig. 11.
Fig. 5.
Fig. 6.

ELEMENTS OF ARCHITECTURE.

PRACTICAL GEOMETRY.

PLATE I.

Fig. 1.—An equilateral triangle, which has three equal sides and equal angles.

Fig. 2.—A triangle with unequal sides, called a scalene triangle.

To describe the figure, the three sides being given:—

Let *ab* be the longest side, *AB*; then, take the length of *ad* in the dividers, and, with one foot on *A*, draw the arc at *D*. Proceed in the same manner with the length *bd*; and, with one foot of the dividers in *B*, make the curve at *D*; through the point of intersection, draw the lines *AD*, *BD*, and the figure is formed.

The equilateral triangle is formed in the same way.

Fig. 3.—A rhomboid, or parallelogram, whose opposite sides are equal and parallel.

Fig. 4.—A rhombus, having four *equal* sides, with two acute and two obtuse angles.

Fig. 5.—An obtuse angle, or one which contains *more* than ninety degrees.

Fig. 6.—An acute angle, or one which contains *less* than ninety degrees.

Fig. 7.—A right angle, or one which contains *just* ninety degrees.

To raise a perpendicular to a given line:—

Let *AB* be the given line, and *D* the centre, making *AD* equal to *DB*; then, open the dividers the distance of *AB*, and intersect the curve lines at *C*. Through the points *C* and *D*, draw the straight line *CD*, and the work is done.

NOTE.—By the term perpendicular it is understood, that any line cutting another line at right angles is perpendicular to that line, let it have what inclination it may. Horizontal means parallel to the horizon.

Fig. 8.—A circle. All circles are supposed to be divided into 360 equal parts, called degrees.

The distance from the centre of a circle to the circumference, is called its radius,—plural radii. The chord and arc of a circle will be understood by a reference to the figure.

Note.—A circle, strictly speaking, is the space included within its circumference.

Fig. 9.—A method of measuring any rectilinear figure.

Let *ABCDE* be the given figure; divide it into the three triangles, *ABC*, *ACD*, and *ADE*, by drawing the lines *AC*, *AD*; then, draw *EF* perpendicular to *AD*; *DH* to *AC*; and *BG* to *AC*.

Multiply *AD* by *EF*, and divide the product by 2; the quotient will be the area of the triangle *ADE*.

Proceed in the same way with all the triangles, and the sum of the several areas will be the area of the figure required.

Fig. 10.—A method of inscribing a circle within a triangle.

Let *ABC* be the given triangle. At the angle *A*, make *Aa* equal to *Ab*; at the angle *B*, make *Ba* equal to *Bp*; at the angle *C*, make *Ce* equal to *Cf*; then bisect *ab*, *ap*, and *cf* in their centres *c*, *d*, and *o*; draw lines from the angles *A*, *B*, *C*, through the centres *c*, *d*, *o*, till they intersect each other, and the point of intersection will be the centre of the circle.

Fig. 11.—An easy method of ascertaining the area of a circle.

Describe a circle of any radius. Let the given radius be *AD*; then, make *AB* equal to the circumference of the circle, and draw the line *BD*, which forms a right angled triangle, *ABD*. Multiply *AD* by *AB*, and divide their product by 2; the quotient will be the area of the circle.

A different method of obtaining the area of a circle will be given in another part of the work.

Fig. 12.—A manner of describing an ellipse by ordinates, the length and breadth being given.

Let *AC* and *BD* be the length and breadth required. With a radius equal to *AE* in the dividers, and one foot in *E*, describe the semicircle *AFC*. Divide *AFC* into any number of equal parts, and draw lines from the points of division at right angles with *AEC*, as at *FED*. Then, draw *BG* parallel to *AC*, and produce the line *GE*. Make *ab*, at *BE*, equal to *ab* at *AG*; and so of all the rest, as at *cd*, *cd*. Trace a curve line through the points where the straight lines cut each other, and the ellipsis will be formed.

Fig. 13.—A method of constructing an equilateral triangle in a given circle.

Let Ag be the radius of the circle, and g the centre.

With one foot of the dividers on A, describe the arc cgd; and from the points where the arc cuts the circumference, draw one side of the equilateral triangle. The other sides are drawn according to fig. 2.

Fig. 14.—Two parallel right lines, AB and CD.

Parallel lines are always equidistant, whether straight or curved.

Plate II.

Fig. 1.—A Roman arch, which is a semicircle.

Fig. 2.—A Saxon arch, in the *form* of a semicircle, the centre of which falls below the springing of the arch.

Fig. 3.—The lancet Gothic arch of the first period of Gothic architecture. It "assumes the outlines of the lancet, or bay-leaf."

The form is simple, and will be readily understood by an examination of the figure.

Fig. 4.—An equilateral arch, which will also be easily comprehended by inspection. This is the arch of the *second* period of Gothic architecture, and is described from abutments of the arch about an equilateral triangle.

Fig. 5.—A depressed Gothic arch, described from centres on the spring-line within the arch.

Fig. 6.—A Gothic pointed arch, described from a given height and given width.

Fig. 7.—A Turkish ogee arch, formed in the mosques of Constantinople.

Fig. 8.—A Tudor Gothic arch, which came into use during the reign of that family.

Fig. 9.—A semi-ellipsis, found in the Norman examples.

The mode of forming the arches mentioned above, will be understood by an examination of the plate, without any further description.

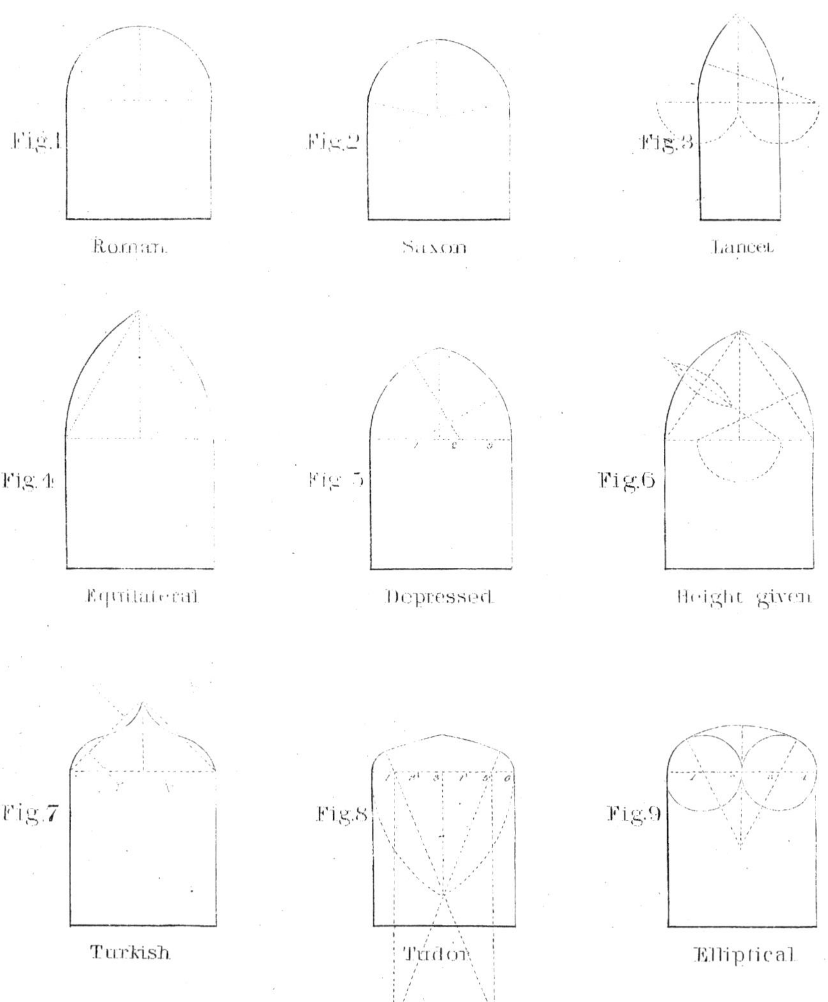
Fig.1
Roman
Fig.2
Saxon
Fig.3
Lancet
Fig.4
Equilateral
Fig.5
Depressed
Fig.6
Height given
Fig.7
Turkish
Fig.8
Tudor
Fig.9
Elliptical

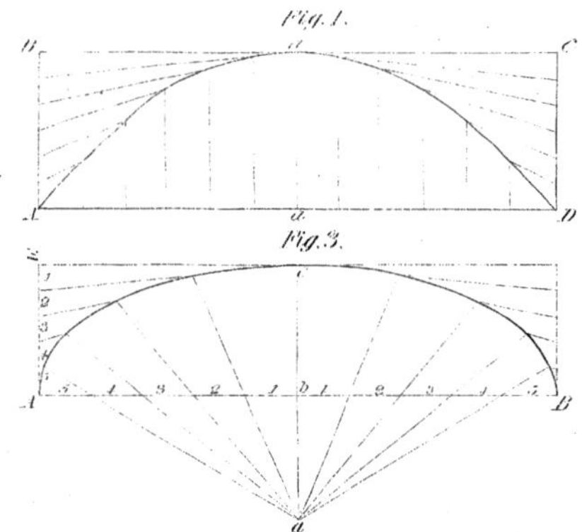

Elliptical Arch.

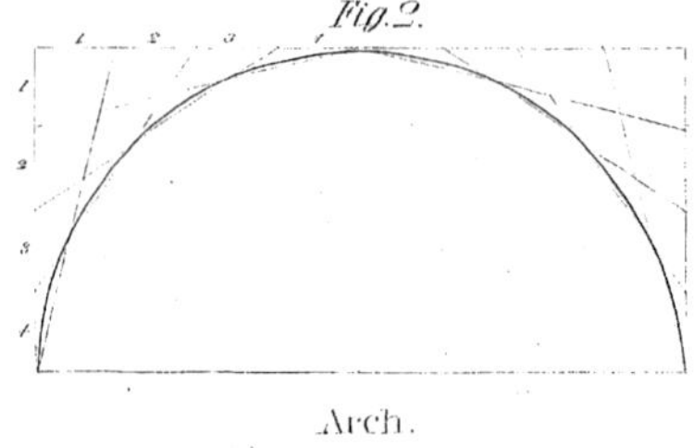

Arch.

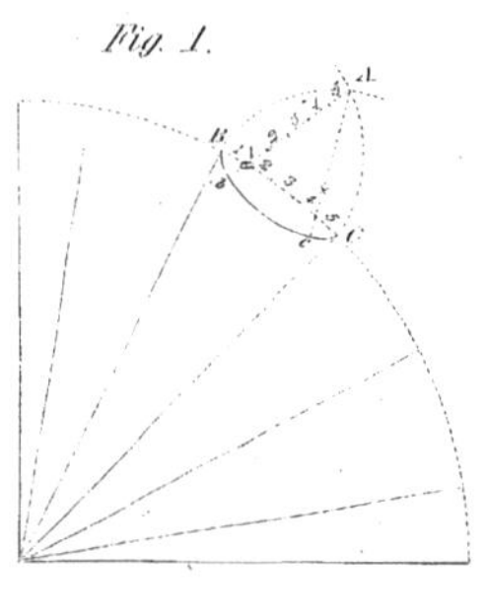

Doric.

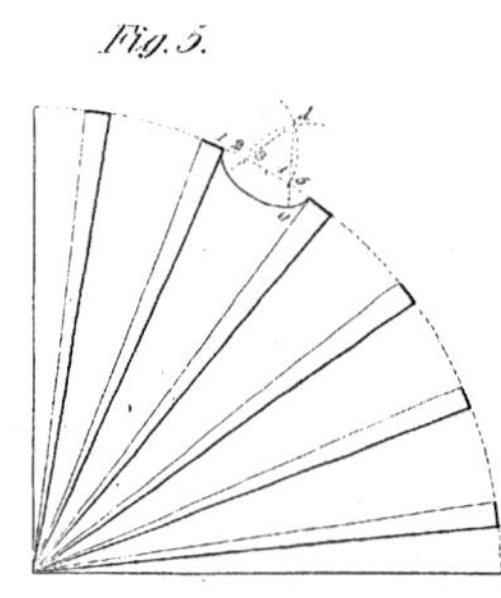

Ionic.

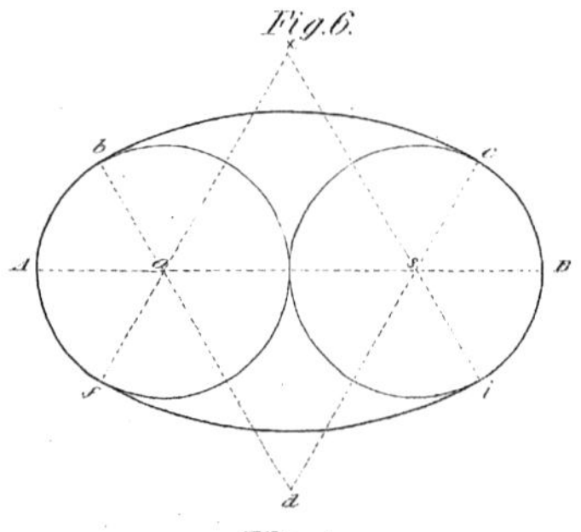

Ellipsis.

Plate III.

Fig. 1.—A method of drawing a parabolic arch, or curve.

Let *AB* be the height required, and *AD* the length or span. Divide *AD* into any number of equal parts with *a* as a centre; and, also, divide *AB* and *CD* each into one half the same number of parts. Draw lines from the point *a*, in the line *BC*, to intersect with the points of division in *AB* and *CD*. Raise perpendiculars from the points of division in *AD*, to intersect respectively the oblique lines above. Then, trace a curve line through these points of intersection, and the figure is completed.

Fig. 2.—A method of describing a semi-circular arch by intersecting lines. Divide the height into as many parts as may be convenient, and half the length into the same number of parts; then draw intersecting lines, as seen in the figure, and trace a curve line through the points of intersection.

Fig. 3.—A method of describing an *elliptical* arch by intersecting lines.

Let *AB* be the given length, and *AE* the height, and make *ab* equal to *bc*. Divide *AB* into any number of equal parts, and *AE* into one half the same number of parts. Then draw the intersecting lines, and trace the curve line as represented in the figure.

Fig. 4.—To divide the Doric column into flutes.

The Doric column should be divided into twenty parts or flutes.—See the figure. Divide one of the parts into five equal divisions, and make *AC* and *CB* equal. Draw lines from *A* through the points 1 and 4, to *c* and *b*, and divide the line *oA* into five equal parts. With one foot of the dividers at 1, on the line *oA*, and the other at *B*, sweep from *B* to intersect the line *Aod*. Proceed in the same manner with the opposite side; then, with *Ad* for a radius, one foot of the dividers being on *A*, describe the curve line *dc*, and the flute is completed.

Fig. 5.—A section of the Ionic column. The fluting of this column is somewhat different from the other.

The shaft of the column is divided into twenty-four parts, and each of these into five other parts.

One of the five parts being taken for the fillet, the four remaining parts will be the flute. The apex at *A* is found with a radius of three parts, one foot of the dividers being at the points 2 and 4.

The first, or side curve, is described by a radius of one part; the remainder by the radius *Ao*.

Fig. 6.—The most simple method of describing an ellipsis.

Let *AB* be the length required. Construct two circles which shall extend the whole distance from *A* to *B*; then, with the radius *so*, describe the equilateral triangle *sox* and *sod*, and draw *xs* to *i*, *xo* to *f*, *ds* to *c*, and *do* to *b*; also, with the radii *SB* and *oA*, describe the arcs *CBi* and *bAf*. Then, with the radii *xi* and *dc*, complete the ellipse, by forming the curve lines *bc* and *fi*.

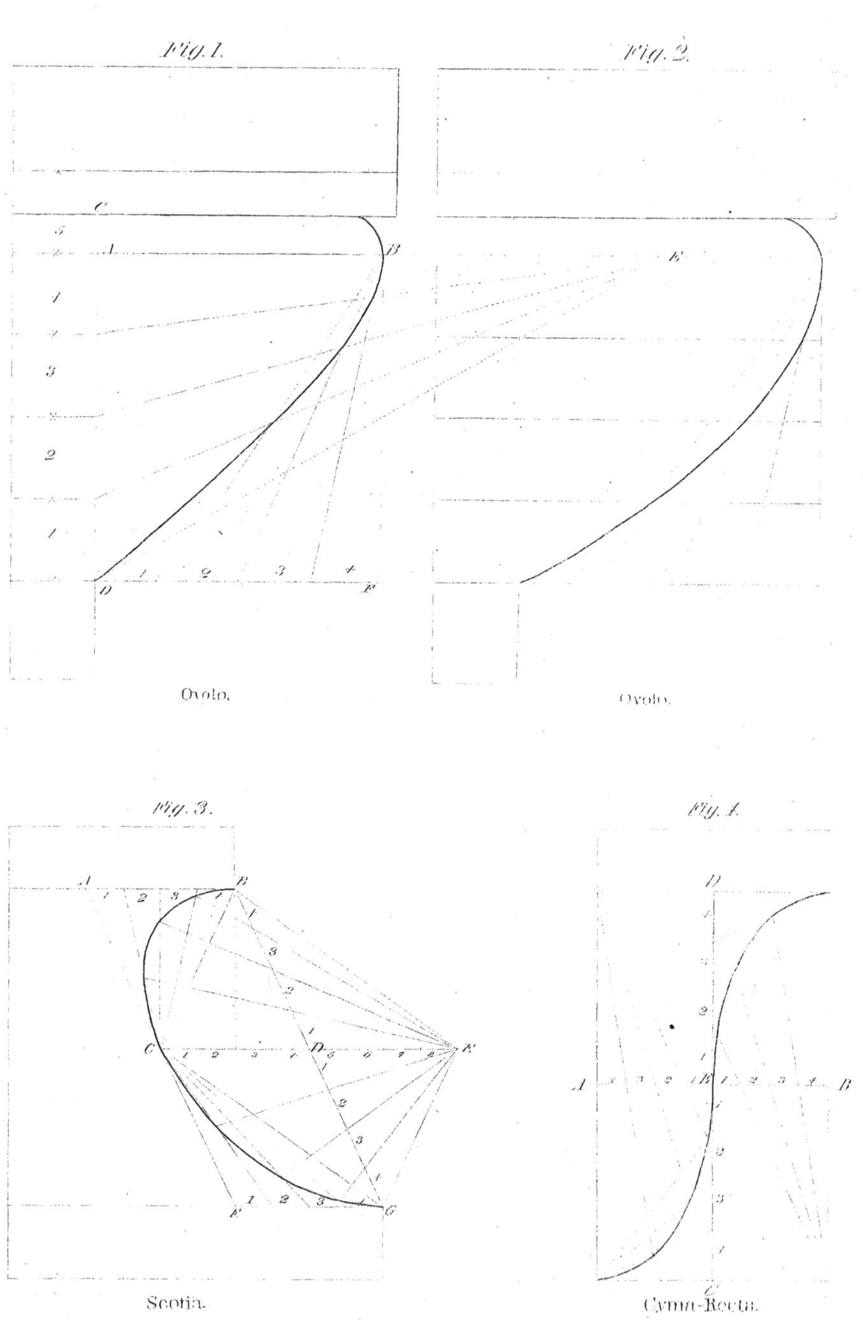
Fig. 1.
Fig. 2.
Ovolo.
Ovolo.
Fig. 3.
Fig. 4.
Scotia.
Cyma-Recta.

Plate IV.

On this plate are exhibited four different mouldings of Grecian form and use, developed from the conic sections.

Fig. 1.—A correct mode of describing a hyperbola, the Grecian ovolo, or echinus.

Let *CD* be the height, and *AB* the projection. Make the quirk 5 equal to $\frac{1}{9}$ of *CD*. Draw *AE* at right angles with *CD*, equal to twice the projection of the moulding ; then, divide *AD* and *DF*, each into an equal number of parts. From the points of division in *AD*, draw lines to the apex *E;* and, also, from the points of division in *DF*, draw lines to *B*. Where these lines intersect each other, trace the curve line *BD*, and the figure is completed.

Fig. 2.—A moulding of the same character, but denominated parabola. This, also, will be understood without a separate description.

Fig. 3.—The scotia of the base of a column. To describe this, let *AF* and *BG* be parallel. Make *DE* equal *CD*, and divide *BD* into any number of equal parts ; divide, also, *AB*, *CD*, *DE*, *DG*, and *GF* into the same number of parts. Then proceed to draw the intersecting lines, and trace the curve as shown in the figure.

Fig. 4.—The cyma-recta, or crowning moulding of the Grecian cor nice.

To describe this moulding, let *AB* be the width, and *CD* the height. Divide it in the centre, both vertically and horizontally, by the lines *AB* and *CD;* then divide *AE, BE, DE,* and *CE,* each into any equal number of parts. Draw right lines through these points of division, and trace the curve as before.

Second Plate IV.

The number of subordinate parts of an order of architecture is eight. The parts are denominated mouldings, and are common to all the orders.

1. The *quarter round*, *echinus*, or *ovolo*. This is formed by a quadrant, or quarter circle, and is of the Roman character. We will here observe, that the Grecian mouldings were all formed from the conic sections ; consequently, no moulding forms any part of a circle. This remark will apply to all the Grecian examples, and it will be unnecessary to repeat it in the explanation of the other mouldings. It is usually found beneath the abacus of capitals, and is commonly placed between the dentils and corona in the Corinthian cornice. It should not be used in situations below the level of the eye.

2. The *ogee, reversed cyma*, or *talon*, appears, like the echinus, to be a moulding suitable for the support of another.

3. The *cyma-recta*, *cyma*, or *cymatium*, appears well designed for a covering to the other members. It is properly used for crowning members, though it is frequently found in the bed mouldings beneath the corona.

4. The *torus*, like the *astragal*, is formed like a rope, and appears to be intended to support the part to which it belongs.

5. The *scotia*, which is placed between the fillets that accompany the *tori*, is commonly below the eye. It is used to separate the *tori*, to strengthen the effect of the other mouldings, and to give variety to the base.

6. The *cavetto*, *mouth*, or *hollow*, is a quarter round, like the *ovolo* inverted, and generally used in cornices.

7. The *astragal* is a small *torus*. It is sometimes called a bead.

8. The *fillet*, *listel*, or *annulet*, is used in every situation, and at any height. It is chiefly used to separate one moulding from another.

The above described mouldings are of the Roman character, and were usually ornamented, more or less, by sculpture. It requires good judgment and skill to ornament an assemblage of mouldings, to give an easy repose and avoid confusion.

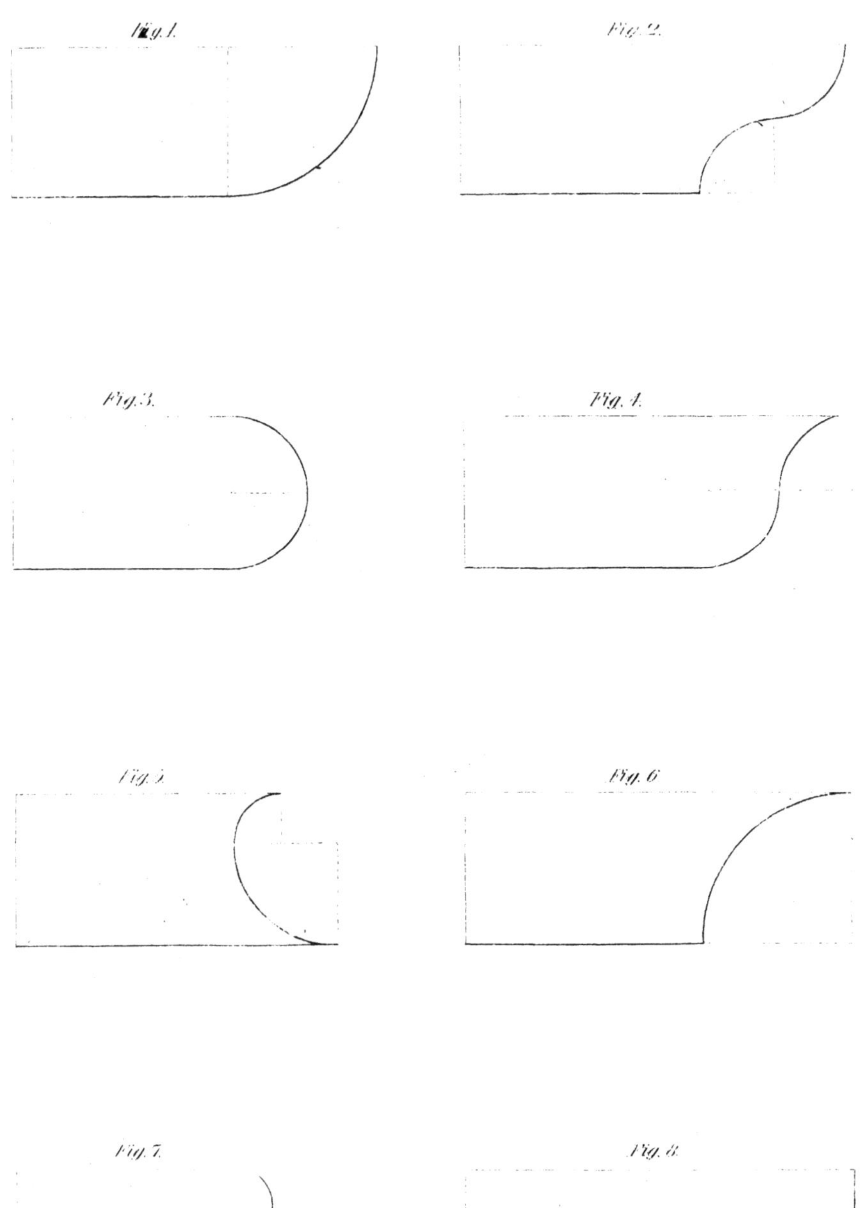
Fig. 1.
Fig. 2.
Fig. 3.
Fig. 4.
Fig. 5.
Fig. 6.
Fig. 7.
Fig. 8.

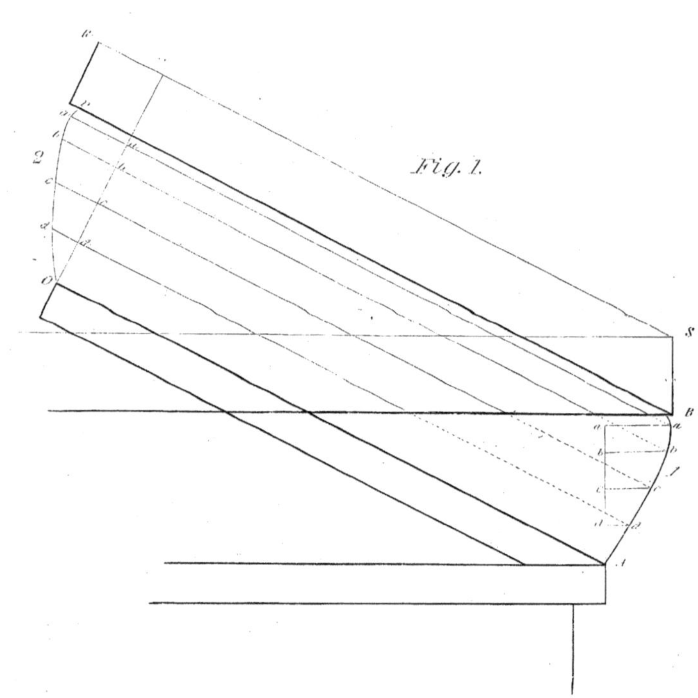

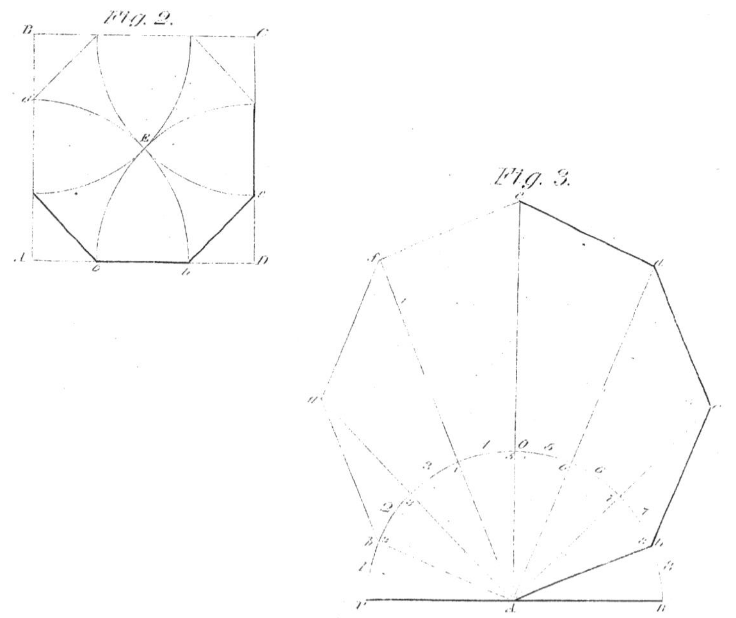

Wm. Brown, Arch.

PLATE V.

Fig. 1.—A method of developing a *raking* moulding from a given *horizontal* moulding. Let *AB* be the given moulding. Divide it, on the curve, into as many parts as necessary, equal or unequal, and draw parallel lines *aa*, *bb*, *cc*, and *dd*, at 1; then, transfer those distances to that part of the figure marked 2, and draw the parallel lines *aa*, *bb*, *cc*, and *dd*. Trace the curve line *op*, and the outline is completed.

After getting the inclination of the roof, *RS*, proceed in the same manner with every kind of moulding, and there will be no difficulty in obtaining a moulding which will perfectly correspond with any other in all its parts.

Fig. 2.—A method of forming an eight-square, or octagon, from a given square.

To describe this figure, let *ABCD* be the given square.

With *AE* for a radius, and one foot of the dividers on *A*, form the curve *ab;* then, with the same radius, and one foot of the dividers on *B*, *C*, and *D*, severally, make the three remaining curves.

Then, draw *be*, which will be equal to *bc;* and so on for all the other sides. The construction of this figure will be evident, without any further demonstration.

Fig. 3.—A mode of constructing an eight-square, one side being given.

Let *AB* be the given side. With a radius *AB*, and one foot of the dividers on *A*, describe the semicircle *BOP*. Divide *BOP* into eight equal parts, and draw lines, cutting *BOP* at 2, 3, 4, 5, 6, 7, and 8, to any indefinite length. Then, with *AB* in the dividers, step round the figure *AbcdefghA*, and the octagon is completed.

To draw a figure with any number of sides, proceed in the same manner, remembering to take more or less of the divisions, according to the number in the figure required to be described.

ORIGIN OF ARCHITECTURE.

The natural wants of the human family, and their necessary protection from the severity of the seasons, gave birth to architecture. From the limited account that is left us, little is known of its infancy and subsequent advancement; but enough to show that it kept pace with the progress of civilization, and that, in proportion as peace was secured, and government established, architecture became no less an object of attention than painting and sculpture. It was another means of transmitting to posterity the degree of civilization to which the nations of antiquity attained. The time that has elapsed since those nations, among whom the art was first introduced and practised, have existed, prevents our examining, with nicety, the peculiarities of their dwellings. We find, however, in the architecture of the ancients, the characteristics of three distinct modes of life, which are discernible even at the present day. The three classes to which we refer, and which, probably, were the only classes into which society resolved itself, were hunters, shepherds, and husbandmen. The first class, being mostly in the chase, sought no better habitations than nature provided for her children; namely, the caverns and holes of the rocks. The second, being compelled to wander from place to place, in order to procure food for their flocks, and possessing more refinement than the former, furnished themselves with tents. These were well suited to their purposes, because they were easy of transportation and sufficiently protected them from the inclemency of the weather. The third class pursued husbandry, and, therefore, required dwellings more adapted to the preservation of their productions. Hence, arose low huts, or wigwams, which, perhaps, were not very unlike those of the aborigines of our own country.

The materials which were used in the erection of the buildings of ancient date, were those most easy of access, and such as the nature of the place and the climate afforded. For this reason, reeds, canes, the leaves, bark and boughs of trees were employed. After some knowledge of the metals was obtained, more substantial materials began to be used; and, in the course of time, articles of an inflammable nature came into disuse, especially in the walls of their public buildings.

Bricks, without doubt, were first employed, having previously been moulded into form and dried in the sun. Then stones; and afterwards, as man became more civilized and learning increased, marble was principally used in the construction of their temples and other splendid edifices.

The construction of the buildings of antiquity needed little skill, and were as simple as the materials of which they were formed. The people possessing less refinement, and being more easily satisfied than those of modern times, had fewer wants to gratify; therefore, they were contented with whatever afforded them a shelter. Accordingly, a few timbers placed above each other, in the form of a square, fastened together at their angles, and covered over with the branches of trees, were all they required.

The architecture of the different countries of the world might with propriety be said to be as different as the people, climate, soil, and productions of the countries themselves; and it would not be improper to give it a name derived from the country which produced it.

For example; the architecture of Babylon, the Babylonian architecture; that of China, the Chinese, &c. But the architecture to which we wish briefly to direct the attention of the reader is that of the Egyptians, to which the present orders of architecture are distinctly traceable.

EGYPTIAN ARCHITECTURE.

There were several characteristic features which strikingly marked the architecture of Egypt, and distinguished it from that of any other country; namely, solidity, strength, and durability.

The temples were built in the pyramidic form, and generally without any roof. The walls inclined inward and enclosed large columns, variously arranged. The most splendid and ornate figures of men, beasts, and birds were wrought in their porticos, architraves, and friezes, which clearly evince a great degree of excellence in sculpture. The entrance to their temples was ornamented with colossal statues, sphynxes, obelisks, &c., and the door-way was surmounted with a winged globe.

A uniformity exists in all the Egyptian temples, and other edifices, which is peculiarly striking; and the repetition of the ornaments was carried to the highest pitch of endurance. The greatest irregularity which has been discovered is that found in the island of Philoe; and this is owing, probably, to its peculiar locality. Among the Egyptians, the arch was seldom if ever used.

The absence of it arose, doubtless, from the desire to preserve a uniformity in the structure of their buildings, or from the want of the requisite knowledge of repairing it when injured. But it is a matter of doubt, whether they possessed any idea of the arch at all.

Its place was supplied by heavy lintils, resting upon large, massy pillars.

The Egyptian column, so far as form was concerned, was either circular, polygonal, or square. Of the first kind, the shaft was sometimes nearly plain, but often highly adorned with hieroglyphics.

Sometimes it represented reeds, bound together at short intervals; and, again, an assemblage of reeds encircled by bands, resembling the hoops of a cask.

Square columns are often found in the ruins of many Egyptian temples, cut from solid stone.

Instead of regular columns, like those we have mentioned above, colossal statues were frequently used to support the superincumbent weight, similar, in some respects, to the Grecian Caryatides.

The Egyptians displayed as great a variety in the use of their capitals as in their columns.

Of these capitals, we notice three, which may be called, according to a distinguished architect, the *square*, the *vase-formed*, and the *swelled*.

The first, in reality, was nothing more than an abacus; but it was often so high as to admit the sculpture of a human head. The second, as its name implies, resembled a vase; the third curved out in the centre; and each of the three was adorned with the most excellent workmanship.

The entablature of the Egyptians, though unlike that in the architecture of Greece and Rome, was very seldom subdivided, or separated into frieze, architrave, and cornice. The pilaster, like the arch, was also wanting in the architecture of Egypt; and windows were not often used. When they were used, they were of the form of a parallelogram, and little ornamented.

The decorations may be considered as belonging to two classes; namely,—those which are alien to the buildings themselves, such as obelisks and statues, and those which are connected with them, and form, as it were, a part,—such as carving on the entablature, bas-reliefs, &c. The first class of these ornaments is distinguished for the size and durability of the materials which compose it.

The statues of colossal proportions, usually in a sitting posture, are detached from the exterior of the temples, and rest on simple pedestals.

Painting was only another method of ornamenting; but the taste exhibited here, as in coloring or drawing, was not better than that displayed in their sculpture.

The leaf of the palm-tree, and plants of almost every kind which the country produced, were carved in the Egyptian capitals. On the entablature and other parts we occasionally find animals of nearly every description, elegantly sculptured; and there is scarcely a building, of any size, where the winged globe is not to be found. The object of the globe, and of all the decorations on the Egyptian temples, was to typify the divine attributes of the Deity, of whom the people had but an imperfect idea.

The exploits of their kings, and large portions of history, were embodied in the sculpture on the walls.

The proportion which is necessary in the different parts of a building in relation to the whole, is not so discernible in the Egyptian architecture as in the Grecian. This disproportion is most distinctly noticed in pyramids and temples.

The private buildings, though less adorned than the magnificent structures which have withstood the ravages of time, are, nevertheless, not destitute of ornament. They varied, of course, in their locality and size.

From this mode of architecture, as we have intimated above, all the orders, namely, the Tuscan, Doric, Ionic, Corinthian, and Composite, can be easily traced.

A description of these orders will be given in the succeeding pages.

GRECIAN ARCHITECTURE.

TEMPLES were the principal structures erected by the Grecians. In order to give the student some idea of the number, magnitude, and distinguishing characteristics of those elegantly enriched and highly ornamented edifices, which were the adornment of Athens and other Grecian cities, we will mention the names of a few of the principal ones.

The chief of the Grecian-Doric examples are, the Parthenon, Temple of Theseus, and the Portico of Augustus, at Athens; the Enneastyle, Hexastyle, and Hypæthral Temples, at Pæstum; the Temple of Juno Lucina, and Concord, at Agrigentum; the Temple of Minerva at Sunium; the Temple of Apollo, and the Portico of Philip of Macedon, in the isle of Delos; the Temple of Jupiter Panhellenius, at Egina; the Temple of Juno, at Samos; the Temple of Bacchus, at Teos; of Apollo Didymæus, at Miletus, and of Minerva Polias, at Priene. We might name others, did our limits permit, but these are sufficient for our present purpose. The last four of these examples are of the Ionic order. The first two in the list, namely, the Parthenon and Temple of Theseus, are the most splendid examples of the Grecian-Doric order.

From the examples here given, we may readily infer that a taste for elegance and grandeur, with simplicity of arrangement and ornament of parts, was cultivated to an extent never excelled, and seldom equalled. This is not surprising, when we recollect that those massive edifices were erected by the joint expenditure of all the Grecian States, and supported out of immense revenues and munificent donations.

The influence of the principles of Grecian architecture stretched along the coast of Asia Minor, entered Egypt, and, probably, followed the conquest of Alexander into India itself on the East, and to the country of Italy and the Sicilian lands on the West.

In the article on Egyptian architecture, we stated that the temples and public edifices of Egypt were decorated with figures of men, beasts, birds, &c., carved upon the frieze, architrave, and walls, and in numerous other places. The same is true in the Grecian architecture; but the temples were not the only buildings in Greece that were enriched by sculpture and art. Many of the monuments, theatres, and tombs were magnificently adorned, as were, also, their fora and stadia.

The ancient temples have been divided into seven classes; viz.—1, in antis; 2, prostylos; 3, amphiprostylos; 4, peripteral; 5, dipteral; 6, pseudo-dipteral; 7, hypæthral.

For a knowledge of these species, the student is referred to Stuart's Antiquities, where he will find an example of each, and its description.

Besides the names we have given above, the temples had other names, depending upon the distance between their columns. The intervening space is called intercolumniation, and is measured by the lower diameter of the shaft. When it is one diameter and a half, it is called pycnostyle; when two, systyle; when two and one fourth, eustyle; when three and one fourth, diastyle; and when four, aræostyle. The eustyle was generally practised by the ancients, and is in use at the present day.

In hypæthral temples, that is, temples whose cells are not covered, columns were sometimes placed within the walls, on the four sides; but, frequently, although within the walls, they were only on the long sides, and took the name peristyle.

Occasionally, the intercolumniation was not regulated by the diameter, but by the triglyphs; and, if only one triglyph intervened, the mode was styled monotriglyph.

This mode was more frequently employed than any other in Grecian architecture.

In the Grecian temples, the number of columns on each flank was one more than twice the number on the front; that is, if there were six columns in front, there would be thirteen on the sides, reckoning the column at the angle in both ranges. The exterior row of columns, with the entablature, standing upon a platform ascended by three steps, entirely surrounded the edifice. The pediments, frieze, and walls beneath the portico, were often wrought with the most excellent sculpture.

Writers on the subject of architecture have so universally considered the hut as a symbol of columnar architecture, which is identical with the Grecian, that, although we have not satisfied ourself in regard to the correctness of the theory, we have not ventured to substitute a new one.

The posts which were driven into the ground to support the roof gave origin, doubtless, to the detached Grecian column. The flutings, or grooves sunk into the shaft of the column, were said to be made for the purpose of affording a place for the spears of persons entering the temples. It is also said that the "folds of a matronal garment" led to their invention. This, however, does not appear to account satisfactorily for their origin, since we are led to suppose that the ancients were acquainted with the fact, that light striking upon a curved surface produces a much greater effect than it does when it falls upon a plain surface. But from whatever source they originated, one thing is certain, they were invented when architecture was in its infancy, and give an additional beauty to the column.

As the ancients wished to build temples with columns, and being ignorant of the proportions necessary to support the superincumbent weight, they resorted to the expedient of measuring the height of a man, and having found his height to be six times the length of his foot, they made application of this fact in the erection of the Doric column, giving it a height equal to six times its diameter. In the temple of Diana, which was built afterwards, on similar principles, they varied the proportion, and made the height of the column *eight* times the diameter, instead of *six*, in order to give it a more lofty appearance. At a later period, the Doric column was made *seven* diameters high, and the Ionic *eight and a half.*

There are several points of difference existing between the Grecian and Roman styles of architecture, which it may be well to state in this connection. The contour of a moulding, in the former style of architecture, was formed from the conic sections; and the contour of a moulding, in the *latter* style, from circles. The dome and arches were found among the Romans, but not among the Grecians; for the columnar style of architecture used by them rendered the arch unnecessary.

The Grecian architects of modern times, however, have endeavored to introduce the Roman arch, with the Greek form of architecture; but, in every case, the attempt has proved unsuccessful.

ROMAN ARCHITECTURE.

It cannot properly be said, that the Romans possessed any original architecture; what they had was little else than a modification of that of Greece.

They were instructed in this science by the Etrurians, a people of Italy, during the reign of the Tarquins. At this time, their edifices were constructed more on fixed principles, and received considerable enrichment by means of sculpture.

The first Tarquin, who was a native of Etruria, after having gained several victories, enjoyed a triumph; and the wealth he obtained from the conquered cities he appropriated to the erection of magnificent temples and halls of justice. During later successful reigns, great additions were made to the knowledge of architecture possessed by the Romans, and, also, many modifications in the construction of their public edifices, and private buildings. We shall not, however, attempt to trace all the different changes and alterations which are to be found in the progress of Roman architecture, for that would extend this chapter very far beyond suitable limits, and encroach upon ground that does not properly belong to a work of this description.

Architecture was but partially understood by the Romans, until their victorious arms had made Greece a Roman province, and then it received a new, if not its first impulse; but it was not till after a succession of victories, that architecture reached its full height, and made Rome, the Eternal City, what it was.

Statues of the most elegant sculpture, and all the luxury of ornament which the age and country of Greece afforded, poured into the Roman villas, which, at this time, were of considerable extent. No decoration which Greek art could furnish was unobserved in the erection of Roman edifices.

The temples of the Romans generally resembled their Greek original; but, occasionally, there was considerable departure from the Grecian style. These deviations, however, were very few, and, in some respects, little calculated to become a favorite, since they did not always produce a happy effect. The most splendid temple of the Corinthian order that ever existed in Rome, and probably in the world, was that of Jupiter Stator, in the Campo Vaccino. Recent discoveries have shown that it was an octastyle peripteral temple, having twelve columns on the side ; and the depth of the cell contained eight columns, with their intercolumniations. The capitol, both in design and ornament, surpassed anything of the kind that had ever been executed before.

Not far from the temple just described, is the Temple of Jupiter Tonans, of the Corinthian order. This was a hexastyle peripteral, and much inferior to the Temple of Jupiter Stator ; this, however, was not without beauty, although, in the cornice, it was very deficient, in comparison with the one just named.

The Temple of Mars Ultor, also built by Augustus, was a fine example of the Corinthian order. Notwithstanding the temples we have mentioned are all of the Corinthian order, we do not intend to convey the idea that the Romans made use of none of the other orders. The whole of the five orders were generally employed by them, but they underwent several alterations in their hands.

THE ORDERS OF ARCHITECTURE.

An order of architecture is a system or assemblage of parts subject to certain uniform established proportions and divisions. The proportions are regulated by the several services or offices which they have to perform, requiring strength. An order may be considered the "genus," of which there are five *species*, namely, the Tuscan, Doric, Ionic, Corinthian, and Composite orders.

The grand divisions of an order consist of a column and entablature; these are subdivided into assemblages, as follows; viz., the base, shaft, capital, architrave, frieze, and cornice.

The Grecians had three orders of temple architecture; namely, the Doric, Ionic, and Corinthian. The Grecian-Doric orders lay claim to the greatest antiquity, and had their origin in Asia. They were invented or composed by the Asiatic Dorians, who, without doubt, borrowed their ideas from the Egyptians, with whom they had intercourse.

THE TUSCAN ORDER.

We begin our description of the orders with the Tuscan, which is considered the most massive.

This order was invented in Etruria, a country of Italy, now called Tuscany; hence, the Etruscan or Tuscan order. "It is formed upon the model of the ancient Doric, with such alterations as suggested themselves to the architects of those days. The chief of these consisted in the alteration of the proportions of the shaft, and in making it plainer, and with a base. It was never fluted, and the column contained seven of its diameters in height."

"It is generally known as the Vitruvian Tuscan."

ROMAN DORIC ORDER.

The Doric order was originally formed by the Dorians, but it was so modified by the Romans as to differ in appearance from the same order employed by the Grecians. In some edifices the shaft was fluted to nearly two thirds its height, with twenty aris flutes, the lower third being left plain; in others the whole length of the shaft was fluted. The column contains eight of its diameters in height, with mouldings at the base.

ROMAN IONIC ORDER.

The Ionic order has less sublimity than the Doric, but more elegance. Its capital is better enriched with ornaments. It is supposed this order was founded upon the imitation of the female form, and that the proportions of the Doric order were obtained from those of the male form.

The base of the column was designed to represent a shoe; and the capital had a curling ornament, called a volute, said to resemble the tresses of the hair, falling to the right and left.

The column is nine of its diameters in height, and has flutes and fillets.

ROMAN CORINTHIAN ORDER.

The Corinthian column is slenderer and more adorned than either the Doric or Ionic, and its elegant capital adds greatly to its appearance.

The column has fillets and flutes, and its altitude consists of ten of its diameters.

ROMAN COMPOSITE ORDER.

The most ornamented of the five orders was the Composite. It was composed from the Corinthian and Ionic, and was much employed in the public buildings of the Roman capital in the reign of Titus. This column also has flutes and fillets, and its altitude is the same as the Corinthian. The frieze is adorned with excellent sculpture.

In concluding our observations on these orders, we quote the following language:—

"According to the rules of true taste, these orders ought never either to be blended or found in different proportions on the same story; nor ought the same order, strictly speaking, to be introduced in two stories of the same building. And where two or more orders are employed in an edifice, the heaviest should occupy the base, surmounted by the others, according to their successive lightness, which contributes the greatest elegance of style, and gives that harmony to the general design, for which the ancients were so particularly distinguished."

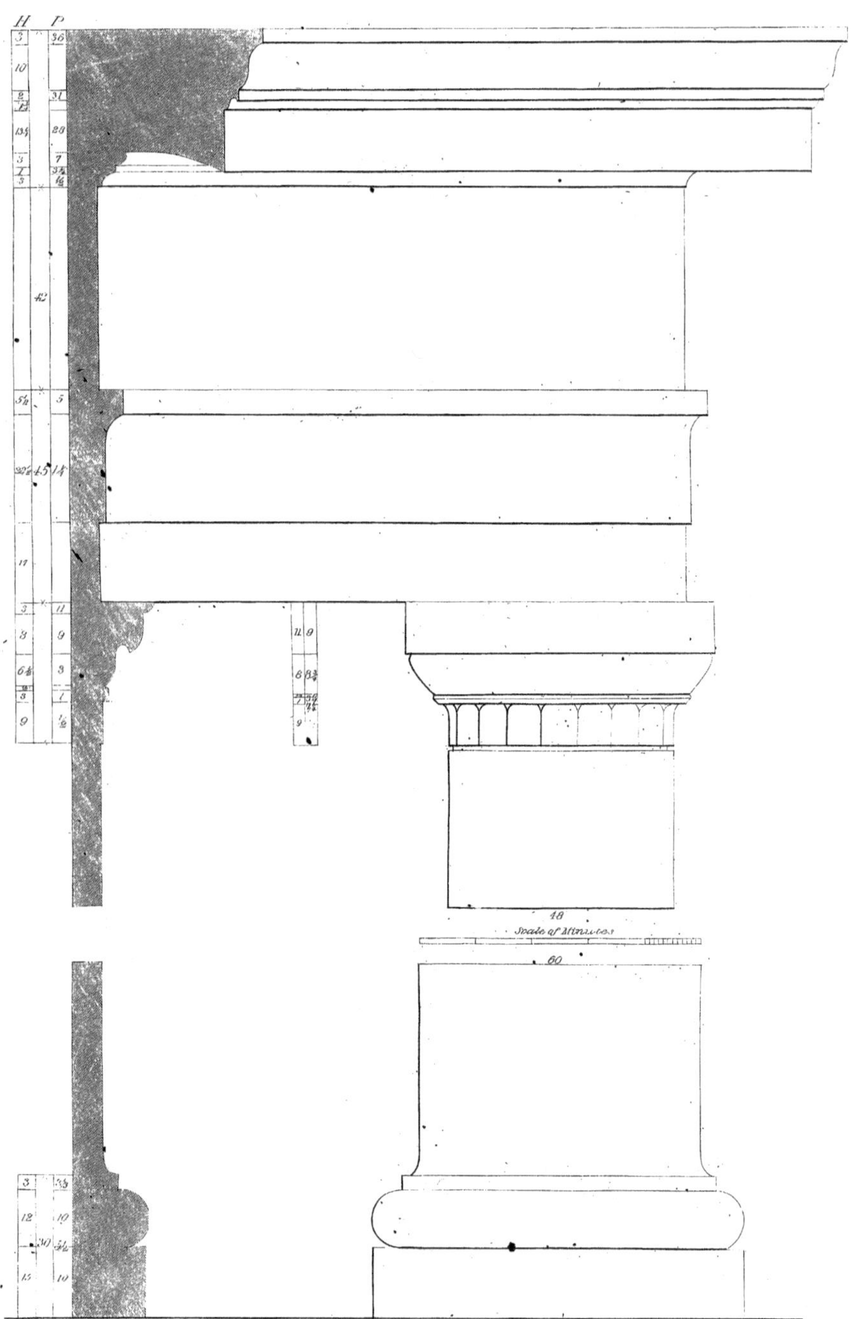
H
P
Scale of Minutes
48
60

TUSCAN ORDER.

Plate VI.

We have here given an example suitable for practice, as approved by Benjamin; and, also, for the purpose of showing how to draw and adapt this order to any required position, the following

RULE.

First ascertain the required height, and divide it into nine equal parts; take one of these parts for the diameter of the column just above the base; this is called the diameter. Make the column, including base and capital, seven diameters high, and the entablature, which includes all above the capital of the column, two diameters high.

To make the subdivisions, minutes, &c.:—

In the first place, take one diameter and divide it into sixty equal parts. This may be done by dividing the diameter, which in the example is $1\frac{7}{8}$ inches, into five equal parts, each being $\frac{3}{8}$ of an inch. Then divide one of these parts into twelve equal parts. This is easily done by dividing one eighth of an inch into four parts, or one sixteenth into two parts.

These divisions, whether large or small, are called minutes. Then, for the height of each member in the order, give the number of minutes marked opposite in the column under *H*, (height); and for the projection, give to each member the number of minutes marked under *P*, (projection.) These projections are given from the face of the frieze in the entablature, and from the outside of the top and bottom of the shaft of the column.

This rule will apply to all the orders, with the exception of a variation of diameters in height. The names of the different grand divisions, given in the example of the Doric order, are applicable to the grand divisions of all the orders.

THE Frontispiece of this work gives a view of the buildings and extensive grounds of Oread Institute, Worcester, Mass.

It was founded by Mr. Eli Thayer, in 1849, as a Female University. Located on a lofty eminence, about half a mile north of the City Hall, and commands an excellent view of the city and the adjacent country. The buildings are constructed of dark slate-stone, and covered with stucco.

PLT. VII

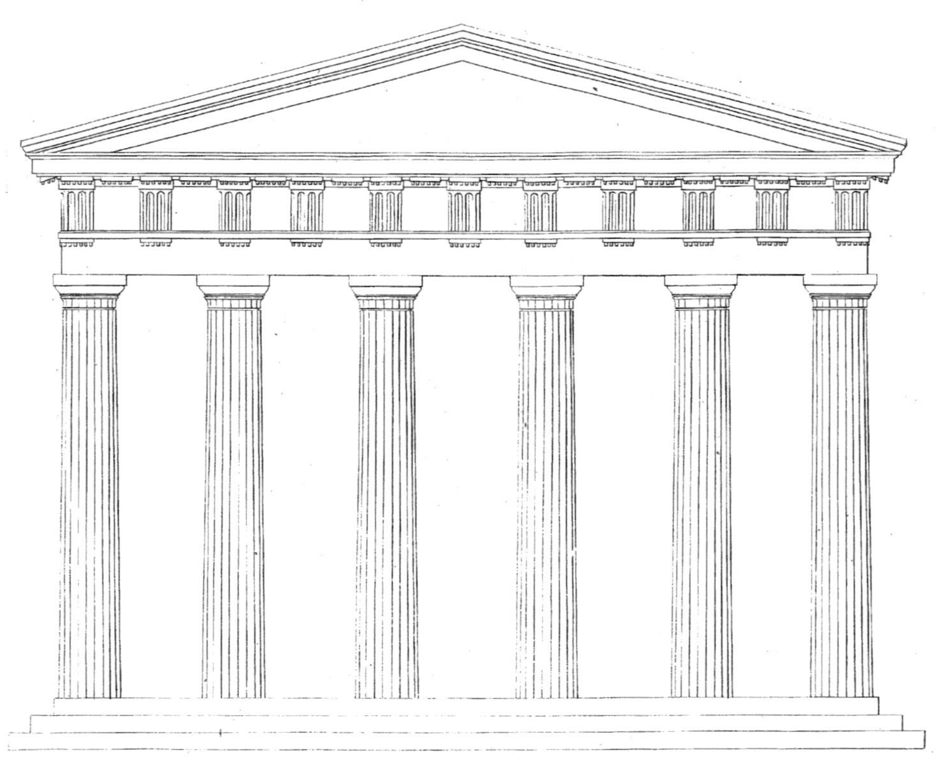

DORIC TEMPLE.

PLATE VII.

ON this plate is exhibited an elevation of a Grecian Doric Temple, in order to give the student a correct idea of the position of all its members. Their names are given on Plate 8.

No. 1.

The front elevation is shown in Fig. No. 1, and is a beautiful design for a house of comparatively small expense.

The following figure, No. 2, is a plan for the arrangement of a flower-garden.

No. 2.

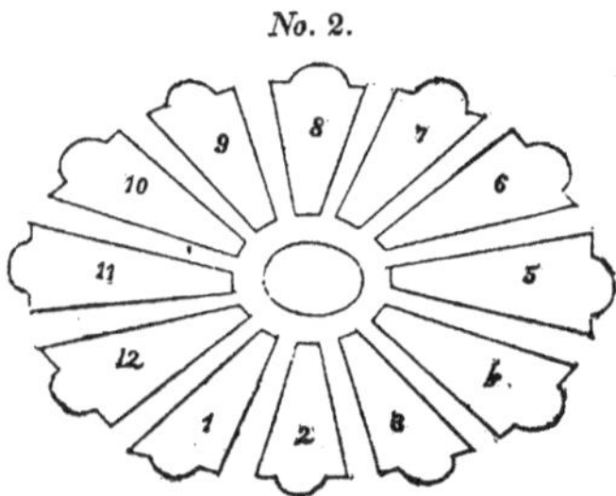

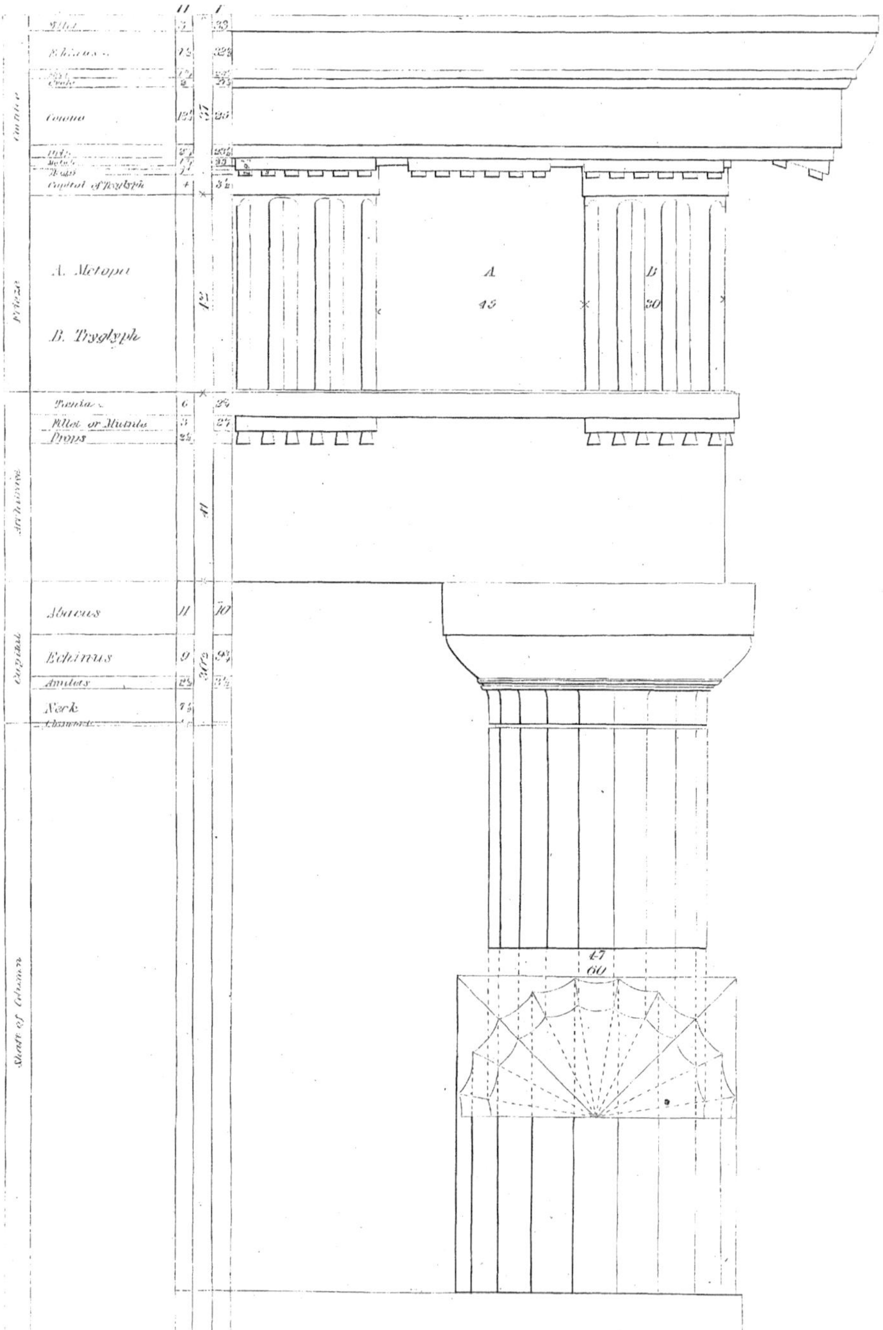

Cornice

Fillet — 3 — 33

Echinus — 7½ — 32⅛

Fillet, Cyma — 1½, 2 — 23

Corona — 12½ — 37 — 26

Fillet — 2½ — 28½

Mutule — 1½ — 33

Drops — 2 — 2

Capital of Tryglyph — 4 — 3½

Frieze — 72

A. Metopa

B. Tryglyph

A 45

B 30

Architrave — 41

Tænia — 6 — 2½

Fillet or Mutule — 3 — 2½

Drops — 2½

Capital — 30½

Abacus — 11 — 10

Echinus — 9 — 9½

Annulets — 2½ — 3½

Neck — 7½

Shaft of Column

47
60

DORIC ORDER.

Plate VIII.

This plate exhibits a part of the column and entablature of the Doric Temple on Plate 7.

This is drawn to the same scale as the Tuscan order, and figured in the same way.

The grand divisions, namely, shaft of column, capital, architrave, frieze and cornice, are marked at the left of the plate; and each of these divisions is subdivided into members, the names of which are given, and their sizes figured in minutes. See the Glossary for the definition of terms used in this work.

No. 3.

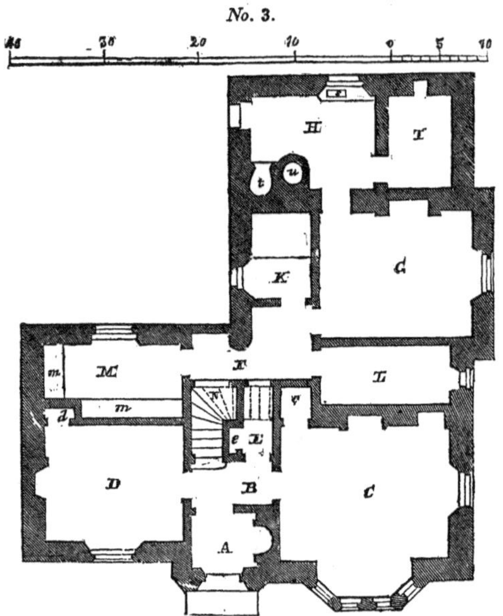

THE ground-plan of the foregoing elevation is seen in Fig. 3. (A) vestibule, (B) lobby, (C) sitting-room, (*c*) closet, (D) parlor, (*d*) closet, (E) passage under the stairs, (*e*) closet, (F) back passage, (G) kitchen, (H) back kitchen or wash-room, (*s*) sink, (*t*) oven, (*u*) boiler, (I) coal or wood-house, (K) bedroom, (L) store-closet, or pantry, (M) milk-room, (*m*, *m*,) stone shelves, (N) closet under the stairs.

No. 4 represents an elegant plan for a summer-house, with rustic columns, around which vines or climbing roses may be trained.

No. 4.

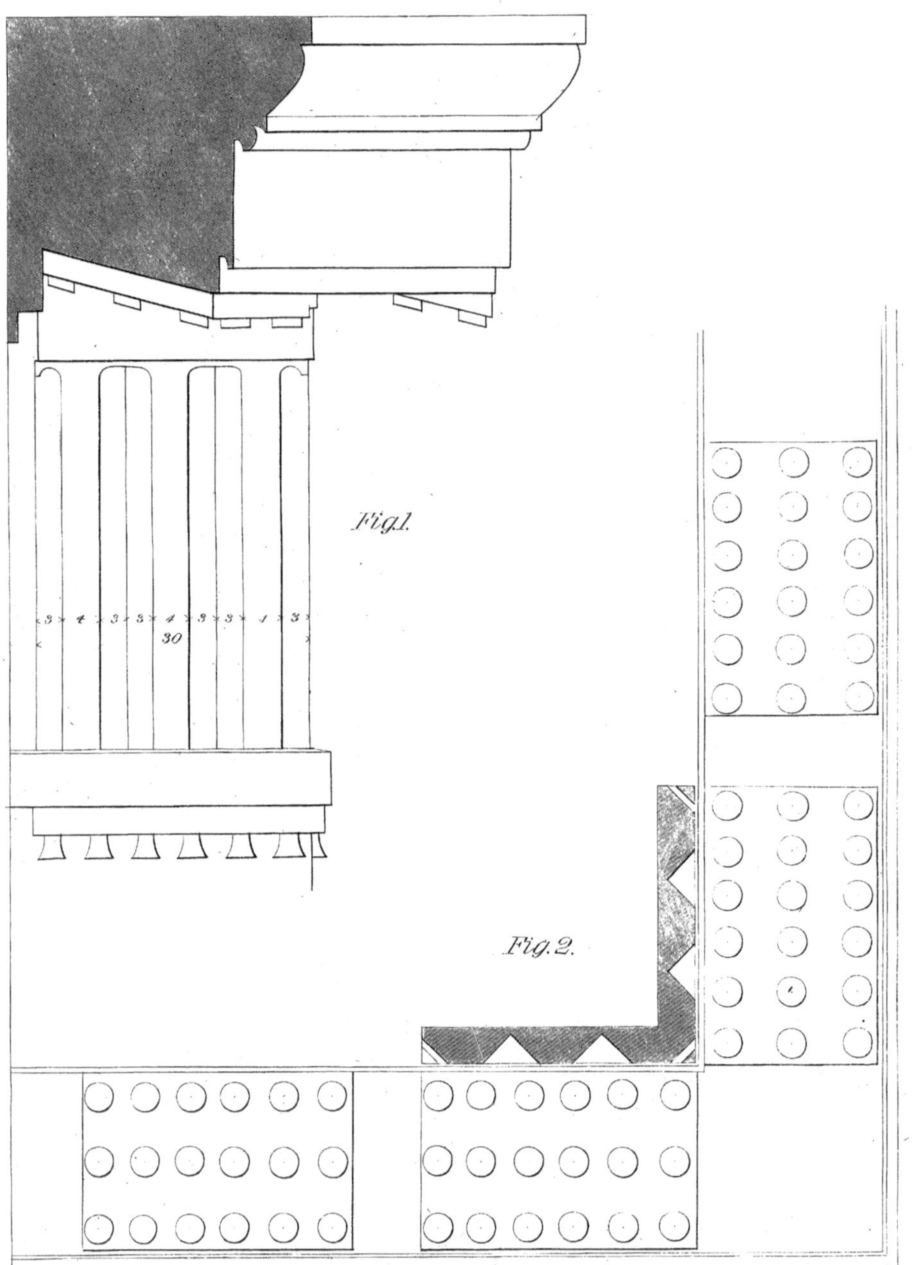

Wm. Brown sculpt.

DORIC DETAILS.

PLATE IX.

Fig. 1.—Sections of the cornice, triglyph, &c.

Fig. 2.—A plancer inverted, also the mutules and triglyphs on a large scale.

For the figuring of this plate, see Plate 8.

The minute on this plate is $\frac{1}{12}$ of an inch; and on Plate 8, $\frac{1}{32}$.

Study and close examination will enable the student to understand this order without any further explanation. We do not intend to give a full and minute representation of all the orders, for this work is designed, more particularly, for practical purposes; but the orders are *shown* merely to give the learner some general knowledge of them, and to enable him to readily make a proper distinction between them.

No. 5.

No. 5, as above, represents a side elevation of the same house.

The upper floor, as seen in No. 6, may be explained as follows: (N) stair-landing, (O, P, Q, R,) bed-rooms, (P) store-closet, (S, T,) also for closets.

No. 6.

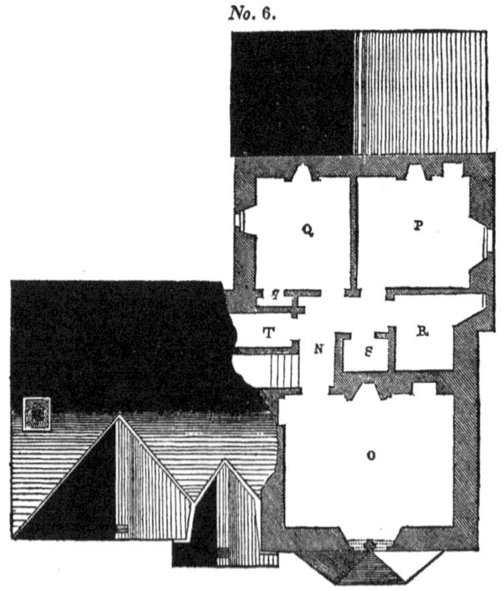

Wm. Brown. Archt.

IONIC ORDER.

Plate X.

This Order owes its rise *to*, and took its name *from*, the Ionians of Asia Minor, who, in their cultivation of architectural taste, introduced into their country the new form which peculiarly distinguishes the Ionic Order, namely, the spiral volute.

This was the second of the Grecian orders in point of time. The column was, as a general thing, made eight diameters in height, always standing upon a base of mouldings, which differs in the outline in different orders. The shaft of the column usually diminishes about ten minutes. The entablature was made two diameters high; the column was divided into twenty-four flutes, each separated by a fillet of one part; the flute consisting of four parts. The capital always maintained the same character, but varied, in form and richness of ornament, in the different examples.

The capitals of the Temple of Erectheus, at Athens, were highly ornamented and very beautiful; while the little Temple on the river Ilissus was very plain; yet its classical beauty and harmony of parts were never excelled.

No. 7.

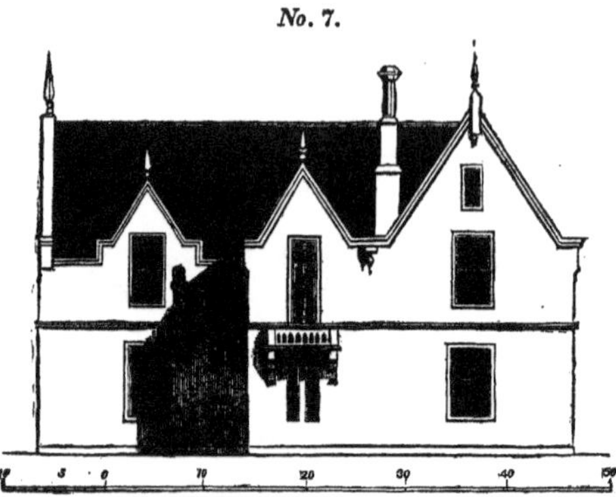

ELEVATION for a large farm-house. The design is seen in No. 7, in which all the main parts of the building are raised to the height of two stories.

The ground-plan is shown in No. 8, as follows: (A) is the vestibule, (B) hall, (C) parlor, (D) sitting-room, (E) dining-room, (F) store-room, (g) stairs, (H) passage, (h, h,) back passage, (I) kitchen, (L) wood-house, (M) milk-room, (N) pantry, (O) closet, (P) closet, (R) closet, (V) kitchen-yard, (T) ash-pit, (S) water-closet.

No. 8.

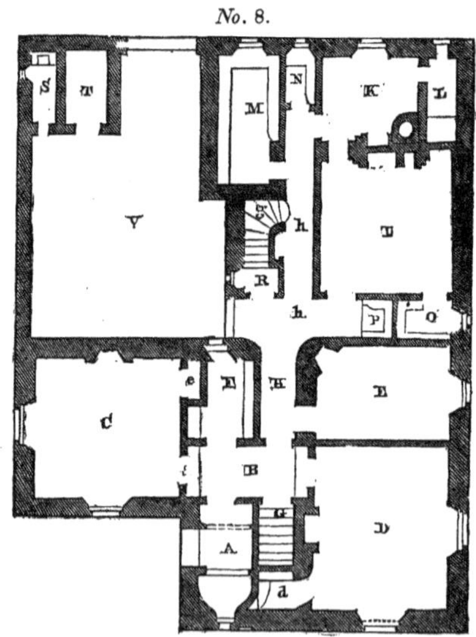

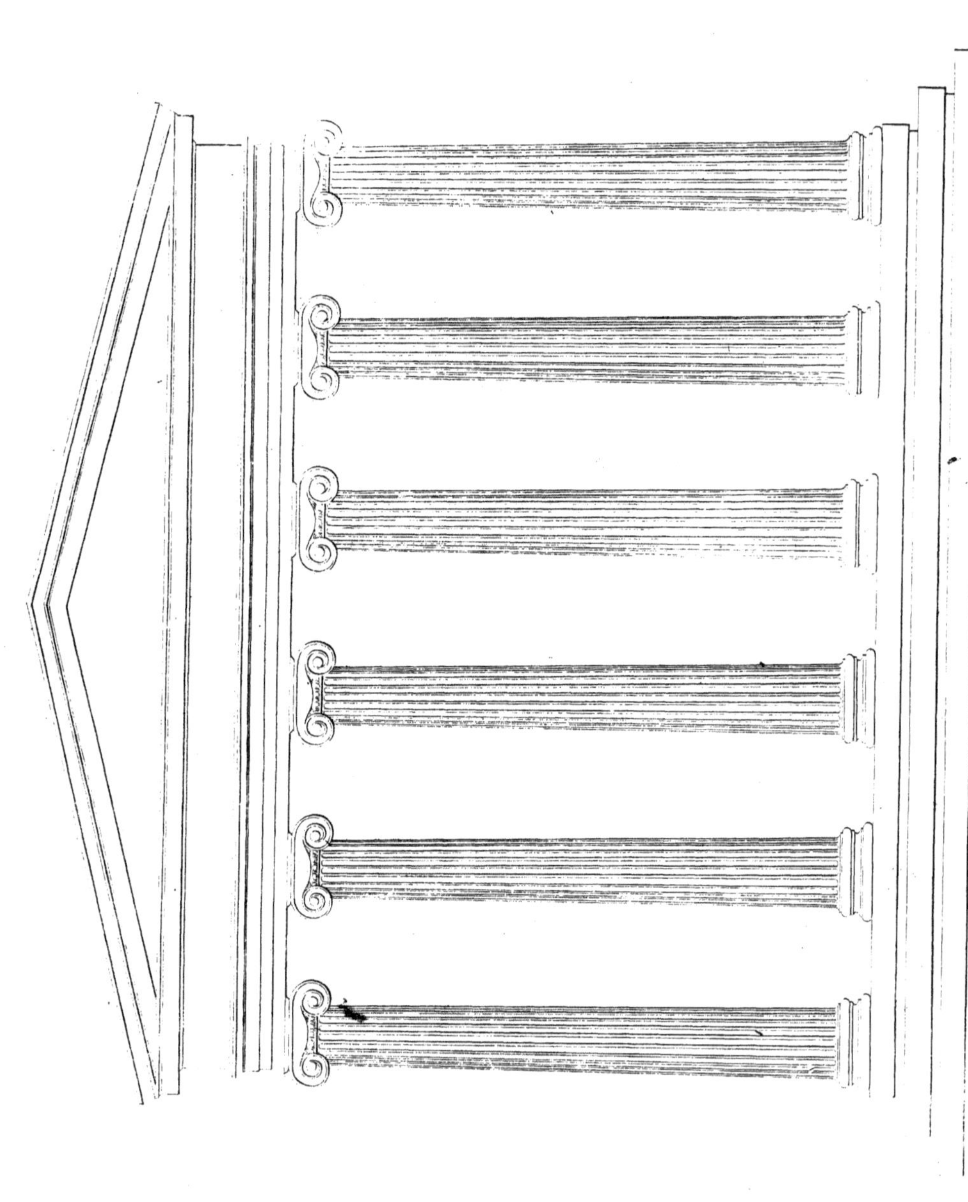

IONIC TEMPLE.

PLATE XI.

ON this plate is represented an Ionic Temple, merely to show the contrast in the different styles of architecture, and to give the student the means of discriminating, at once, between the several orders. This is drawn to the same scale as the Doric Temple, Plate 7.

No. 9.

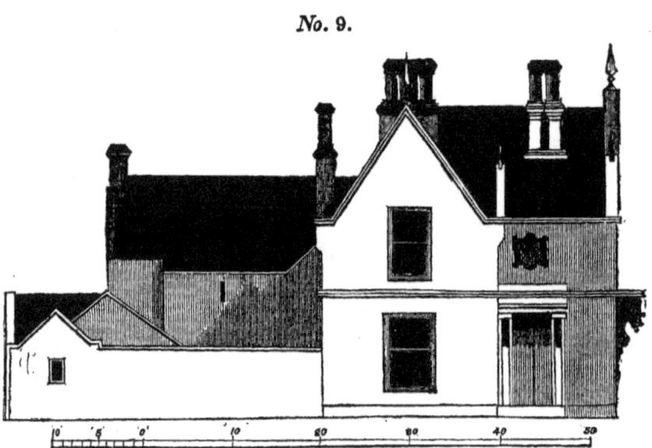

No. 9, as above, represents the side elevation of the same house, as seen in front elevation No. 7.

The upper floor is shown in Fig. No. 10. (B) stair-landing, (A, E, P, K,) bed-rooms, (g) principal stairs, (H) passage, (c) dressing-room, or room for various purposes, (g) back stairs, (n) closet, (L) bed-room (I) closet, (h) landing of back stairs.

No. 10.

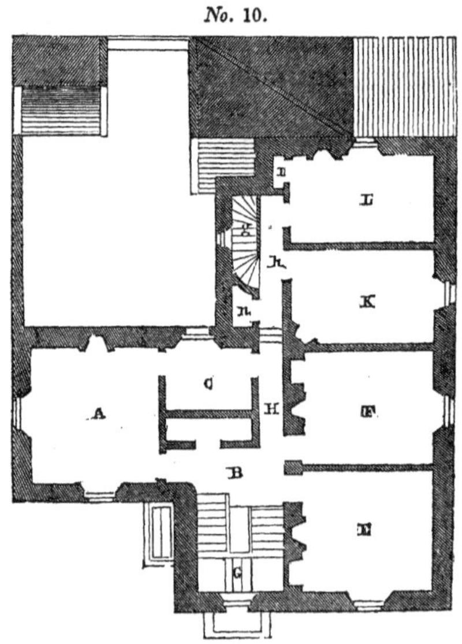

PLT. XII.

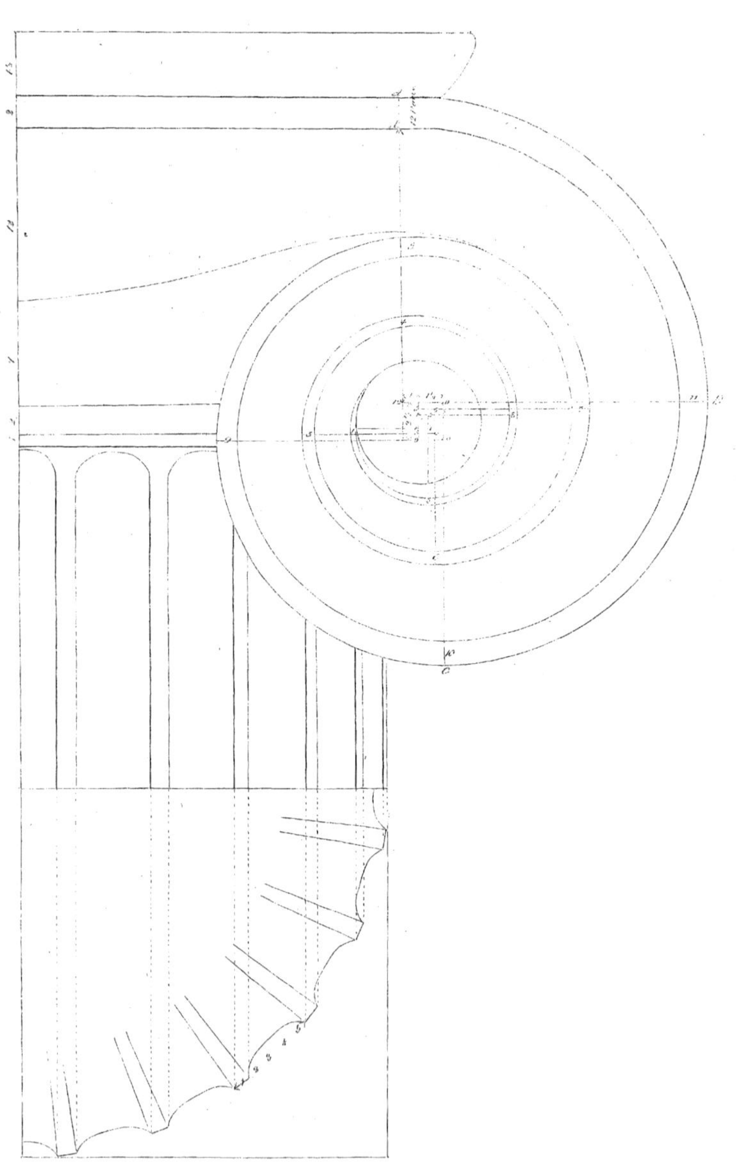

IONIC DETAILS.

Plate XII.

Shows the volute and a section of the column. A minute here is $\frac{1}{10}$ of an inch The numbers 12, 11, 10, and so on down to 1, are centres. Take 12 as a centre and sweep from *A* to *B*; with 11 as a centre, sweep from *B* to *C*; and so on, till the volute is completed.

No. 11.

TIMBER VILLA, IN THE GOTHIC STYLE.

THIS building is now in process of erection, from the design and under the superintendence of the author, in the city of Worcester, Mass., and designed for the residence of Benjamin Butman, Esq.

The Fig. No. 12 is a design adapted for a flower-garden.

No. 12.

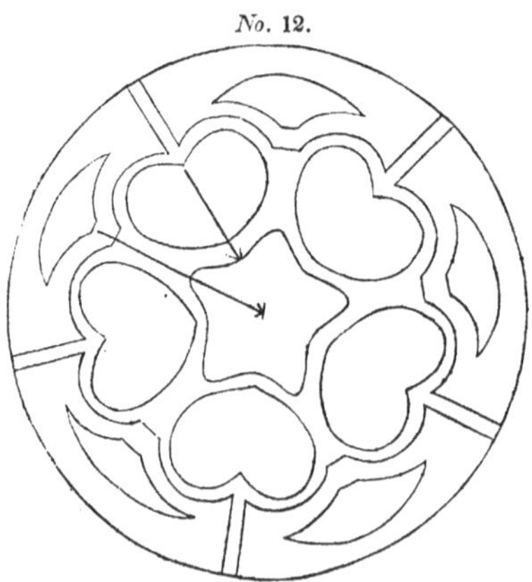

Wm. Brown. Archt.

CORINTHIAN ORDER.

Plate XIII.

The Corinthian was the last order invented by the Greeks. It was seldom employed in their public edifices; and how often in their private buildings, it is not easy to determine. After the subjugation of Greece by the Romans, this order became a favorite with the latter, and its beauty greatly enhanced by an addition of new members, and a further embellishment of costly sculpture.

The fanciful story of Callimachus, which asserts that the acanthus gave origin to the ornament of the Corinthian capital, is too romantic to bear the test of criticism.

Fine examples of this order must be sought in Rome rather than in Greece. The portico and arch of Hadrian, at Athens, are not to be compared to the three columns of the Temple of Jupiter Stator; and the specimens of Grecian art, which have withstood the hand of time, give less satisfaction to the artist, than those beautiful and elegant structures which were the ornament of Rome.

On this plate is shown a Grecian example of the arch of Theseus, or Hadrian, at Athens.

No. 13.

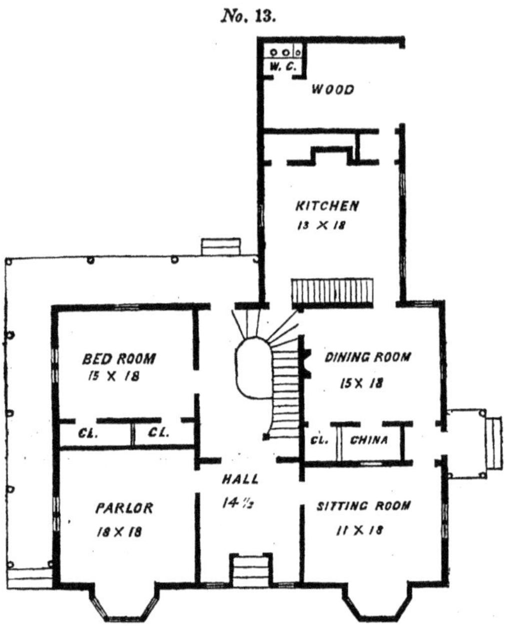

THE above shows the ground-plan of the foregoing elevation, No. 11. The construction of this villa, though simple, is somewhat peculiar. It is framed in the usual manner, with girts one foot eight inches between centres, and sheathed vertically. The sheathing does not exceed ten inches in width, and the joints are covered with battens two and one half inches in width and one and three eighths inches thick, with the two outer corners covered out. The corner-posts, middle girt-beams, and plates, also the rafters to the gables and beams, are furred out four inches, and the corners splayed, as will be perceived by examining the elevation. The rafters project three feet in a horizontal line from the plate, and are planed and covered. The roof-boards that cover the projection are planed and faced down. The principal story is ten feet in the clear; the chambers, nine feet in the clear; front hall, 14½ × 10½; rear hall, 14½ × 20½; parlor, 18 × 18; sitting-room, 16 × 18; bed-room, 15 × 18; kitchen, 15 × 18; china-closet, four feet six inches by six feet; wash-room, eighteen feet six inches by fourteen feet, with all the necessary closets, wood-room, &c.

Estimate the cost of this house to not vary much from $5000.

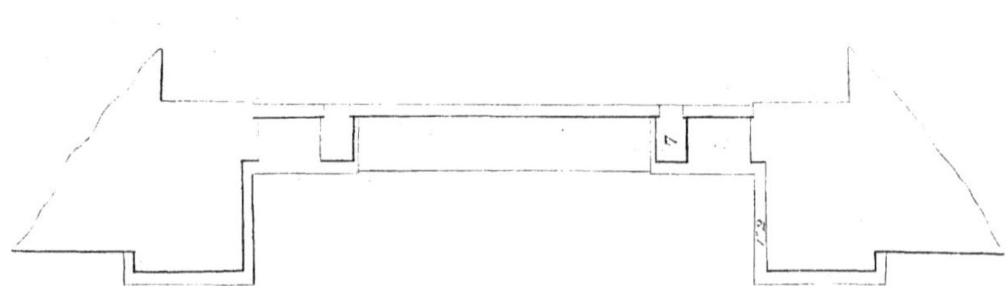

FRONTISPIECE.

Plate XIV.

On this plate is given a design for a Frontispiece with a plan annexed, which is figured in feet and inches. This design, if executed according to the details, will present a fine appearance ; and the carpenter need have no fears in carrying out this plan to the letter. The door is designed to have panes of glass inserted in the panels, which will produce a very pleasing effect.

No. 14 is an elevation of part of a verge-board, to a scale of one inch to one foot.

No. 14.

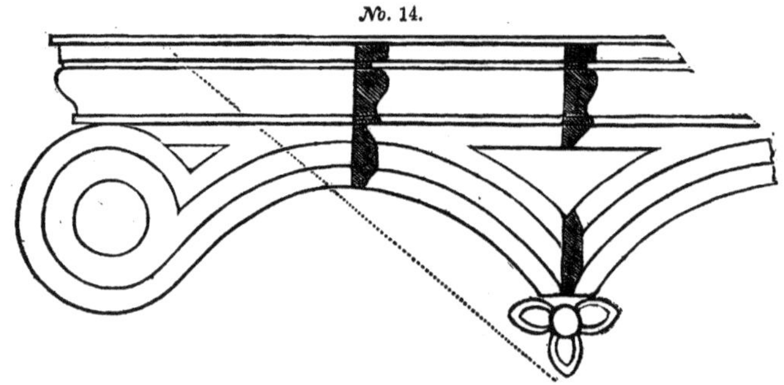

No. 15.

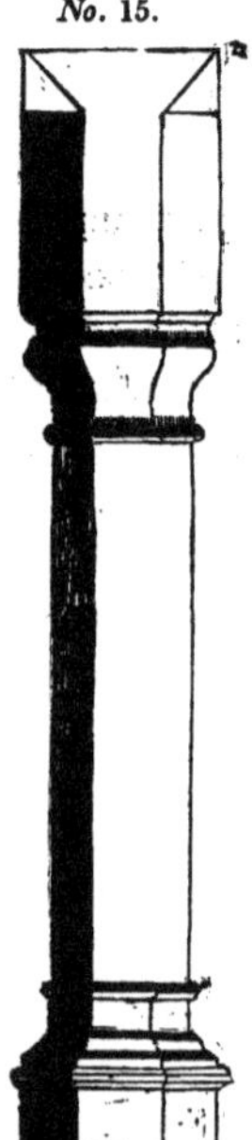

CHIMNEY-TOPS.

EVERY chimney, or stack of chimneys, to be truly architectural, should be treated as a column, or as a group or series of columns; and as every column consists of three parts,—a base, a shaft, and a capital,—so ought every chimney-top. An example of this is shown in Fig. No. 15. Every person that has a house designed for him should object to every chimney-top, whether Grecian or Gothic, that does not consist of an obvious base, shaft, and capital; and the base ought in general to be somewhat higher than the ridge of the roof. In general, all the upper terminations of the building should be bold and free; and this cannot be the case with chimney-shafts, unless they have a distinct base, a shaft of considerable length, and a capital consisting of several members, according to the style of architecture employed.

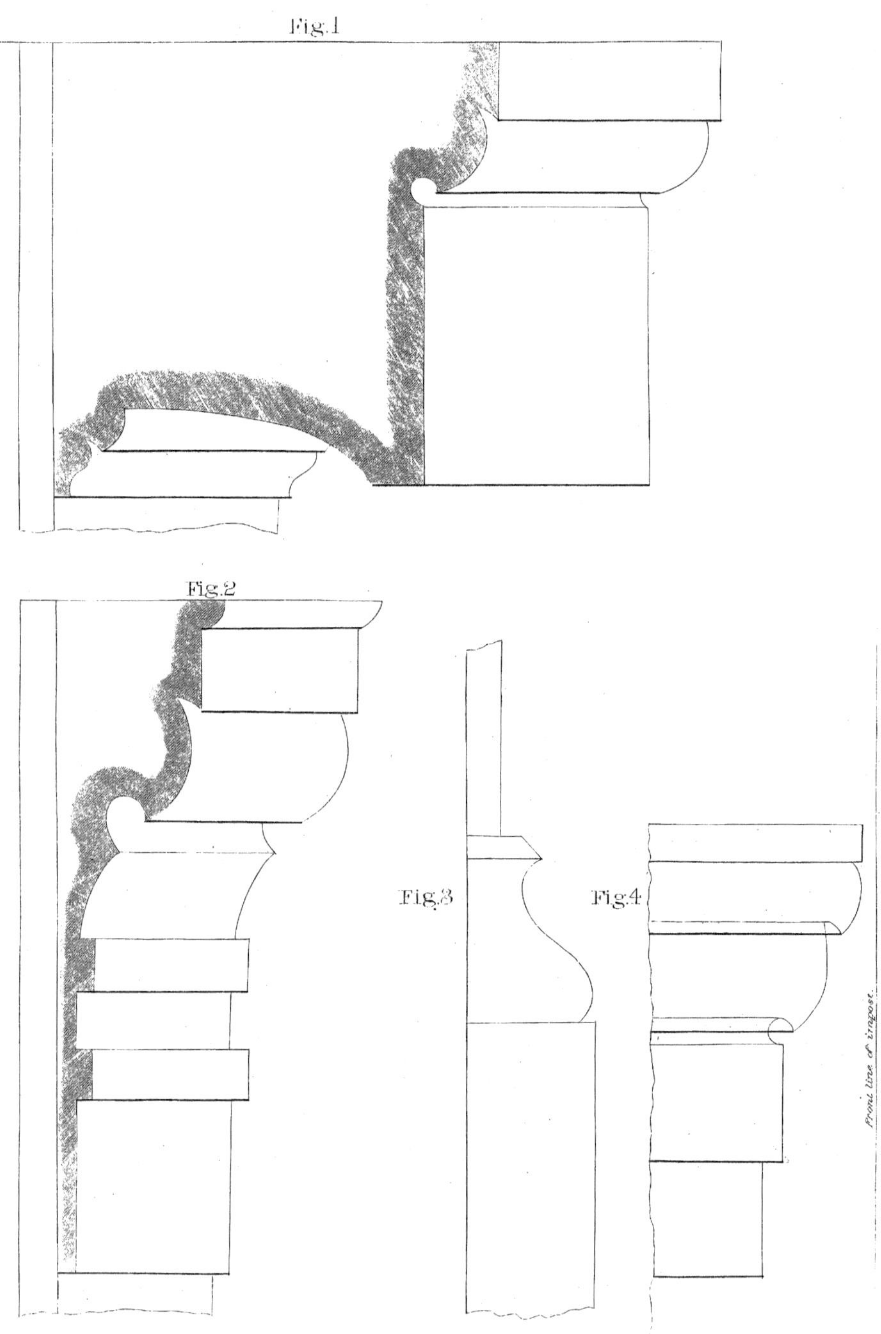

W. R. Emery Eng.

DETAILS OF FRONTISPIECE.

PLATE XV.

THIS plate gives the details of the Frontispiece, (Plate 14,) one half their real size. They will be readily understood by inspection of the Plate. *Fig.* 1, cornice. *Fig.* 2, capital. *Fig.* 3, the base. *Fig.* 4, lintel.

No. 16.

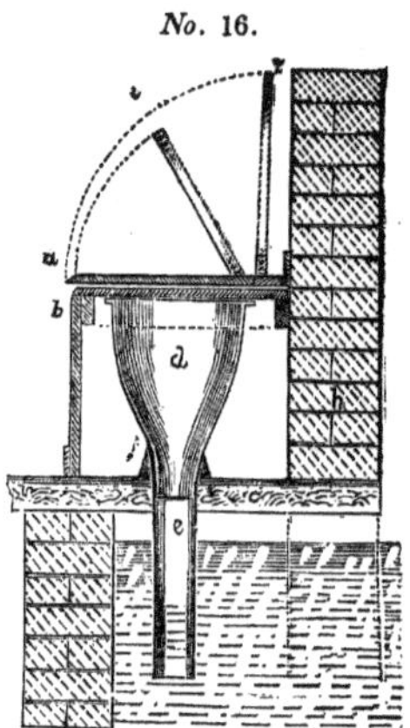

CONSTRUCTING A COTTAGE PRIVY, IN CONNECTION WITH A CESS-POOL OR TANK FOR LIQUID MANURE.

THE privy may be either partially or wholly over the tank, which should be closely covered, on a level with the privy floor, by a flag-stone, as shown in Fig. No. 16. In this figure, *a* represents the seat, which is hinged, in order that when the slops of the house are being thrown in, the seat may be lifted up to keep it from being wetted; *b* shows the fixed and permanent seat, on which the movable seat, *a*, rests; *c* shows the movable seat partially raised up; (*i*) the cover to the whole, raised up; *d* the basin of stone-ware, cemented at *f* into a tube, (*e*), also of stone-ware, or it may be of wood or metal; *g* is the surface of the water in the tank, higher than which it can never rise, in consequence of a waste drain; and it will only fall lower than the bottom of the tube, *e*, when the tank is nearly empty; *h*, *h*, the walls of the tank, and of the back of the privy.

7"8
6
4
4
7
4
4
7
4
3"6
13
13
6
Ft.

FRONTISPIECE.

Plate XVI.

On this plate is given another example of a Frontispiece, which differs somewhat from the former, though not enough to require separate details. It is richer, and will, perhaps, produce a *more* pleasing effect than the first. At any rate, it will give a variety.

No. 17 is a section of the liquid-manure tank, supposed to form also the tank for the privy. In this figure, (*a*) represents the liquid, (*b*) a pierced slate or grating, through which the liquid filters into the well (*c*); (*d*) a bell-trap to admit of the drainings of the yard, and to prevent the risings of smells; and *e* the covering of flag-stone and earth. On a level with the surface of the water in the well, (*c*), there is an opening to a small waste drain, which, as it can only be entered by filtered liquid, cannot readily be choked up. The sides and bottom of the tank and well should be built in Roman cement.

No. 17.

PLATE XVII

WINDOW.

PLATE XVII.

THIS plate shows the inside of a Window and its finish. It is designed for common practice; and, though simple, it is graceful in its proportions. On the right hand side is seen a section of the architrave, and the sizes of each member figured in inches.

No. 18.

GARDENER'S COTTAGE.

No. 18 presents the elevation of a design for a cottage, the interior of which would be found very convenient, and can be built at a moderate cost.

The ground-plan in No. 19 shows (A) entry, and stairs to upper floor; (B) wood-room; bed-room 11 × 12; kitchen 11 × 12, in which there is a closet; pantry, 5 × 8; parlor, 12 × 14; sitting-room, 12 × 14.

No. 19.

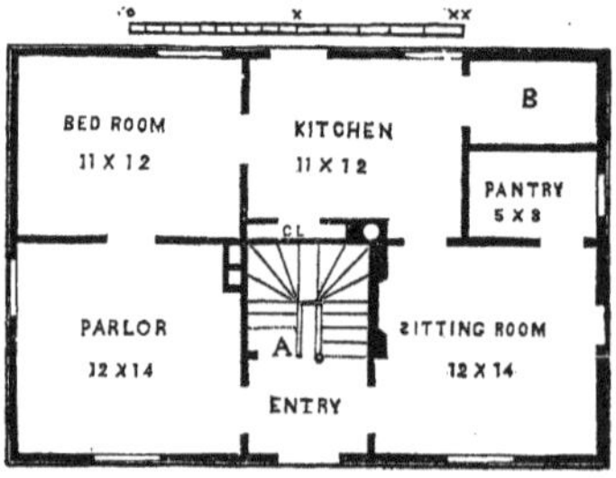

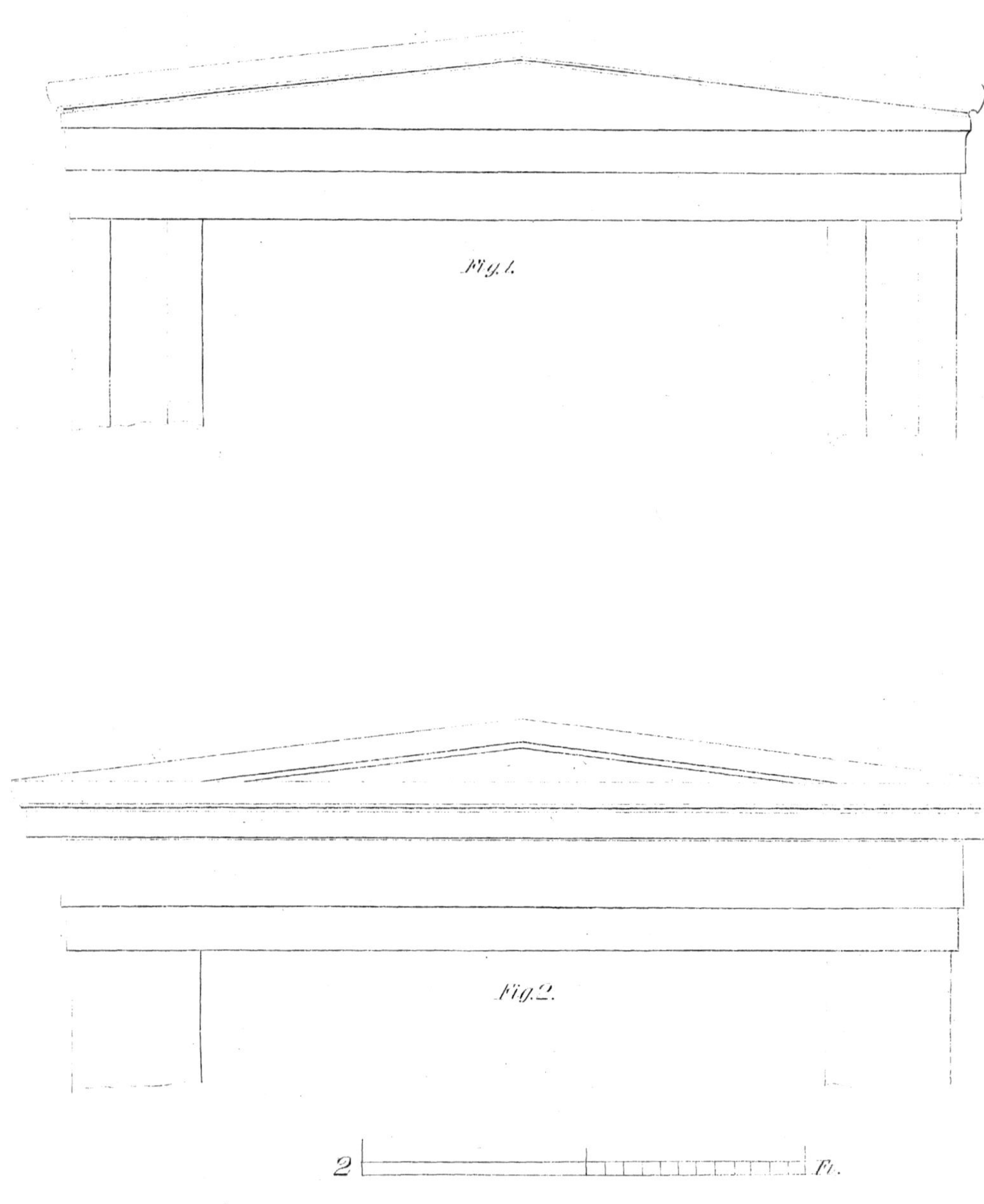

Wm. Brown, Archt.

WINDOW CAPS.

PLATE XVIII.

ON this plate are represented two designs for external window finish.

Fig. 1 has no cornice, except a crowning moulding.

Fig. 2 has a small cornice and a pediment.

No. 20.

MODERN VILLA.

THE elevation is represented in Fig. 20, and the ground-plan in No. 21, which shows an entrance-porch (*a*), hall (*b*), sitting-room (*c*), parlor (*d*), staircase, with closet under, (*e*), kitchen (*f*), water-closet (*g*), back entrance (*h*), pantry (*i*), wash-room (*k*), and wood-room (L).

The staircase is lighted from the tower, and there may be a borrowed light, either from the staircase or the passage to the water-closet, which, being completely within the house, is less likely to be injured during severe frosts.

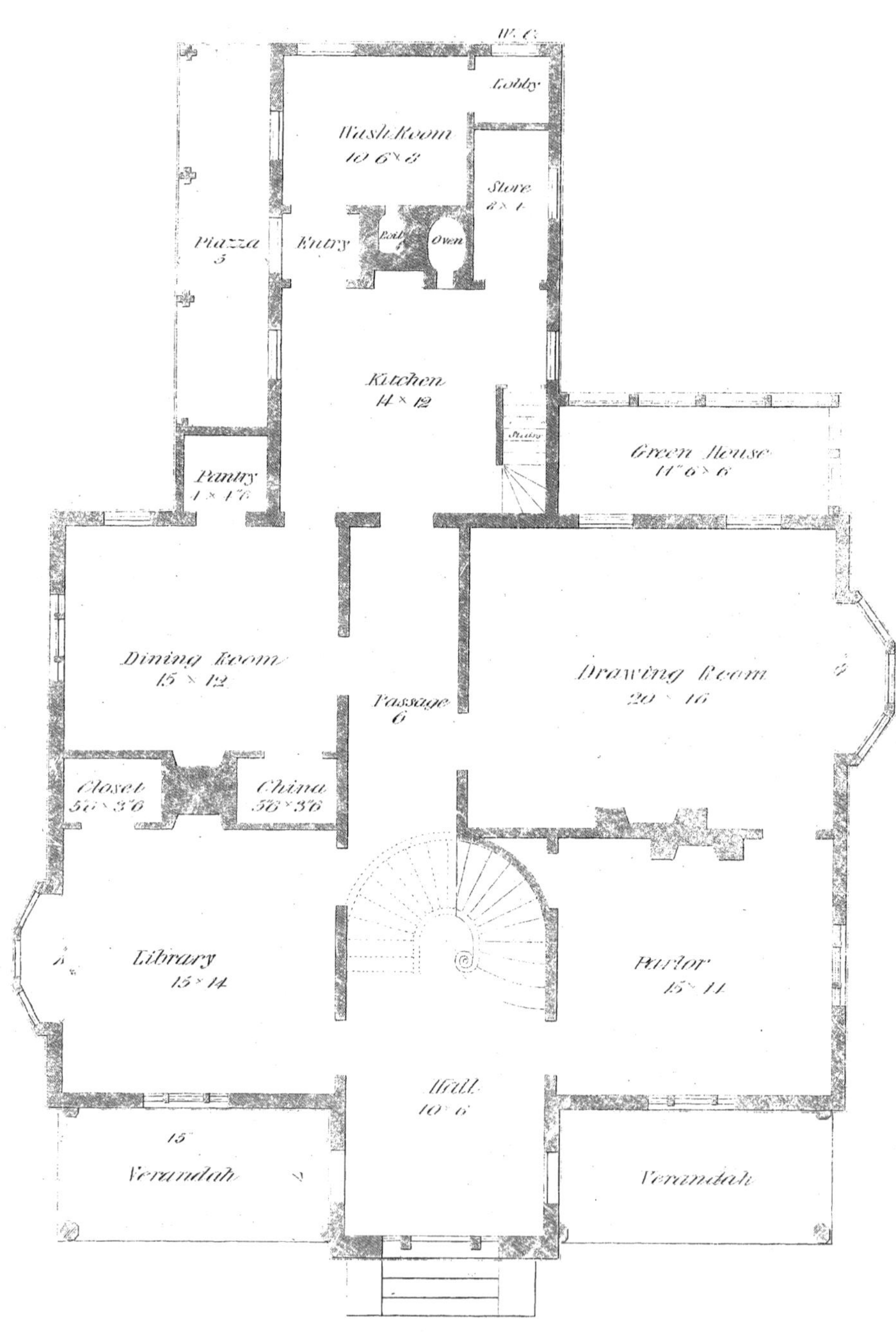
W. C.
Lobby
Wash Room
10 6 × 8
Store
8 × 4
Piazza
5
Entry
Oven
Kitchen
14 × 12
Stairs
Green House
11 6 × 6
Pantry
4 × 4 6
Dining Room
15 × 12
Drawing Room
20 × 16
Passage
6
Closet
5 0 × 3 6
China
5 6 × 3 6
Library
15 × 14
Parlor
15 × 14
Hall
10 × 6
15
Verandah
Verandah

PLAN OF AN ITALIAN VILLA.

PLATE XIX.

WE here present a ground plan of a modern Italian Villa, with the front elevation and details in the succeeding plates. The only apology we have to offer, in giving three designs for dwelling houses in different styles of architecture, is, that there is, in almost all the works upon the subject, a want of adaptation of the various parts to particular places. This is a want that has been seriously felt, even among the more intelligent part of that class of industrious and useful artisans—the carpenters. The design here given is rich in detail, and symmetrical in all its parts; it possesses every convenience usually found in this class of houses. We have not only labored to give expression of *form*, but a full expression of *design*, or *purpose*. And in the attempt we flatter ourself, that we have so far succeeded as to meet the wants of a class of gentlemen, whose means and republican principles will not admit of their erecting more classical or regal edifices.

No. 21.

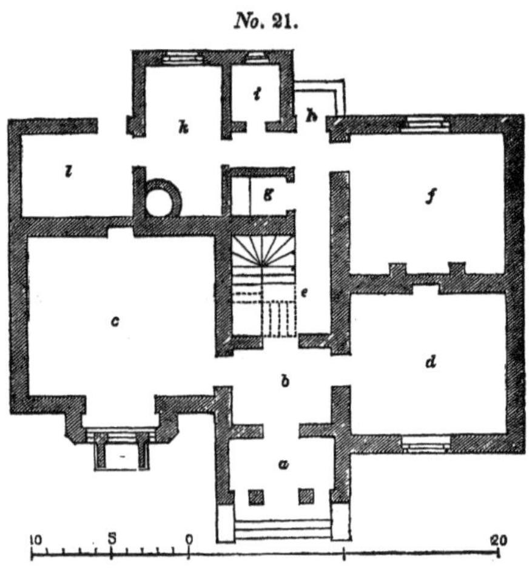

No. 22.

MODEL OF A CHEAP DOUBLE COTTAGE.

The front elevation, as seen in No. 22, exhibits two cottages in juxtaposition, which shows each as having a single family room, or kitchen, on the lower floor, and sleeping apartments above. The cottage, in place of containing one room below, may contain two.

The ground-plan, No. 23, shows (A) the front entrance, (B) kitchen, (*a*) recess for bed, (C) pantry, (*c*) oven, (D) closet, (E) stairs to upper floor, (*e*) closet, or cellar under the stairs.

DES. I.

PLT. XX.

FRONT ELEVATION.

Plate XX.

This plate represents the front elevation of an Italian Villa, which will be understood in connection with the details, &c. It is drawn to a scale of one eighth of an inch to a foot.

No. 23.

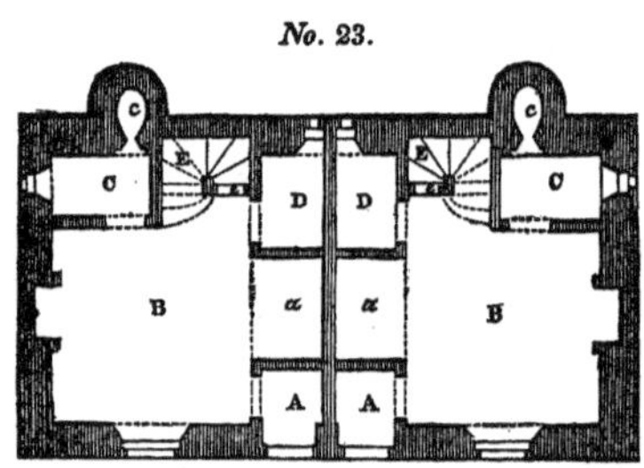

No. 24.

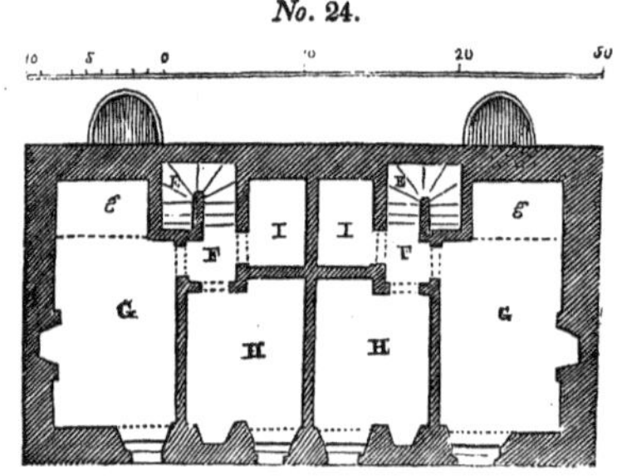

The upper floor of the foregoing plan is represented in No. 24. (F) the stair-landing, (G) bed-room, (*g*) recess for bed, (H) bed-room, (*i*) closet.

Fig. No. 25 represents a ground-plan, suitable for a moderate-sized farm-house. From the entrance and staircase, A, there is a kitchen, B, with wash-room, *c*, and pantry, D; parlor, F; sitting-room, E; store-room and cellar, *g*. The three small apartments, H, I, K, may be used as store-rooms for some of the smaller implements, or as a water-closet, work-shop, &c.

On the second floor there are three bed-rooms, one above the kitchen, and the others above the front rooms, with a dressing-closet over the entrance. The apartments on each side of the kitchen have lean-to roofs, and are not carried to the height of the other parts of the building.

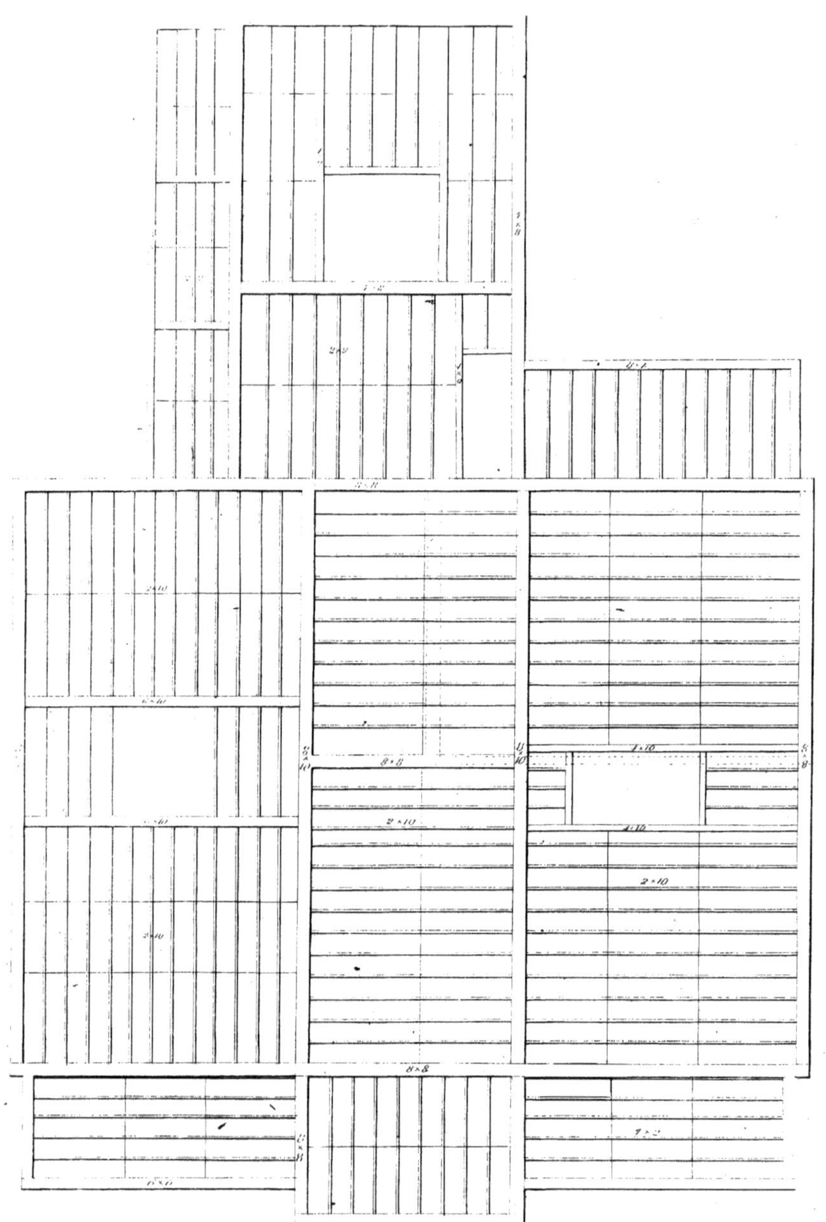

Wm. Jackson, Arch.

FLOOR FRAMING.

Plate XXI.

This plate is designed to show a framing plan of the ground floor, for the Italian Villa. The timbers are all properly represented, and their sizes marked.

No. 25.

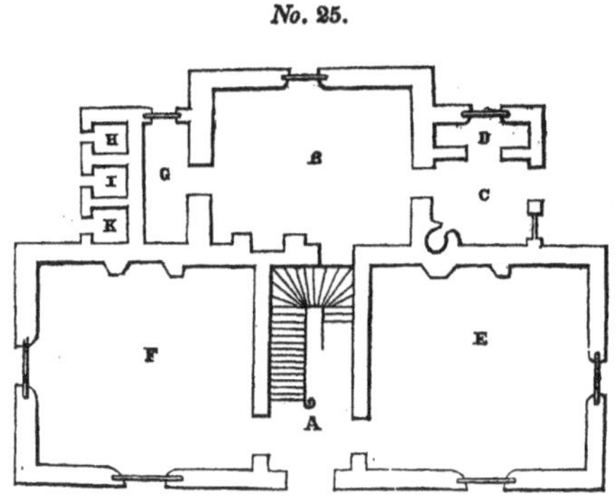

No. 26.

GOTHIC COTTAGE.

THE front elevation exhibits a perspective view of two fronts.

No. 27 represents an elevation of part of a verge-board, to a scale of one inch to one foot.

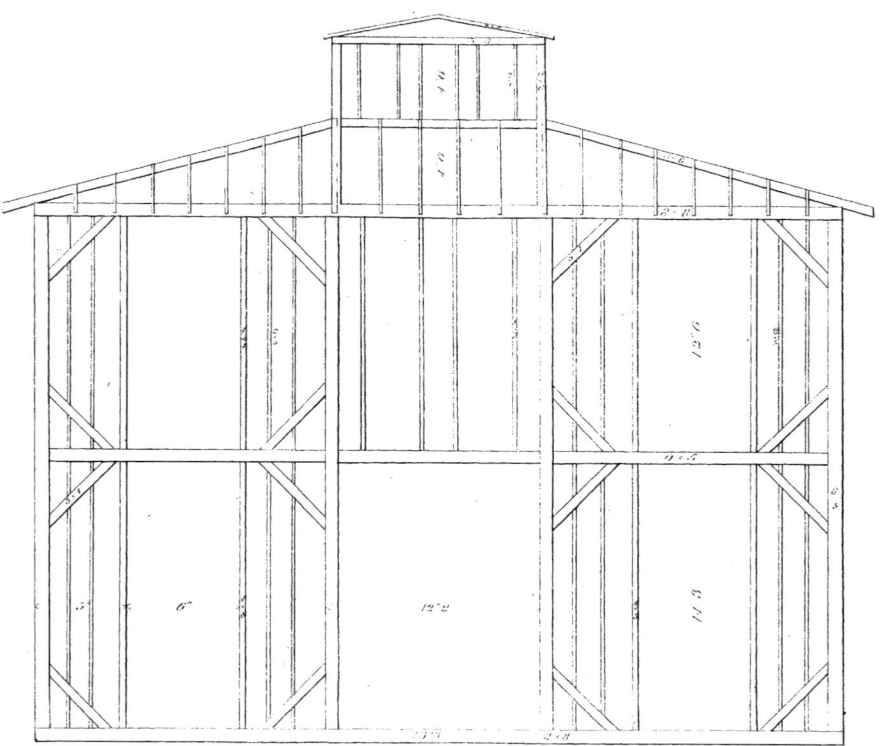

ELEVATION OF FRAME.

Plate XXII.

On this plate the front elevation of the framing is represented. The timbers here are marked, distances and heights given, &c.

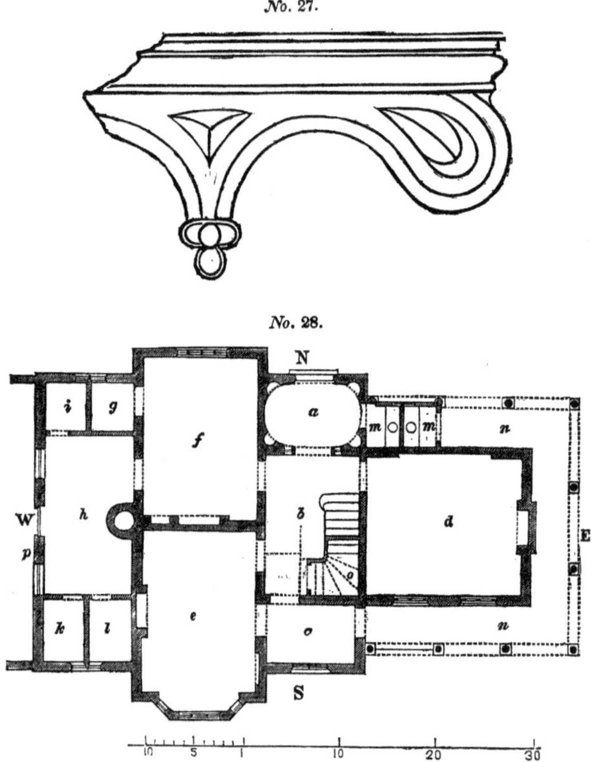

No. 27.

No. 28.

The No. 28 shows the ground-plan, in which *(a)* is the principal entrance porch, which is to be finished with a covered roof, and to have Gothic niches in the angles for statues, or vases for flowers.

From this we pass to the hall and staircase, (*b*), by a Venetian door, the upper part of which may be glazed with stained glass; thence to a small ante-room, (*c*), which, if having a good southern exposure, may be used as a conservatory for plants; from which there is a door to the covered piazza, (*n*). From the hall we enter the sitting-room, (*d*), the two windows of which may be brought down to the floor, and open like French casements, so as to admit of easy access to the piazza, when the ante-room is occupied.

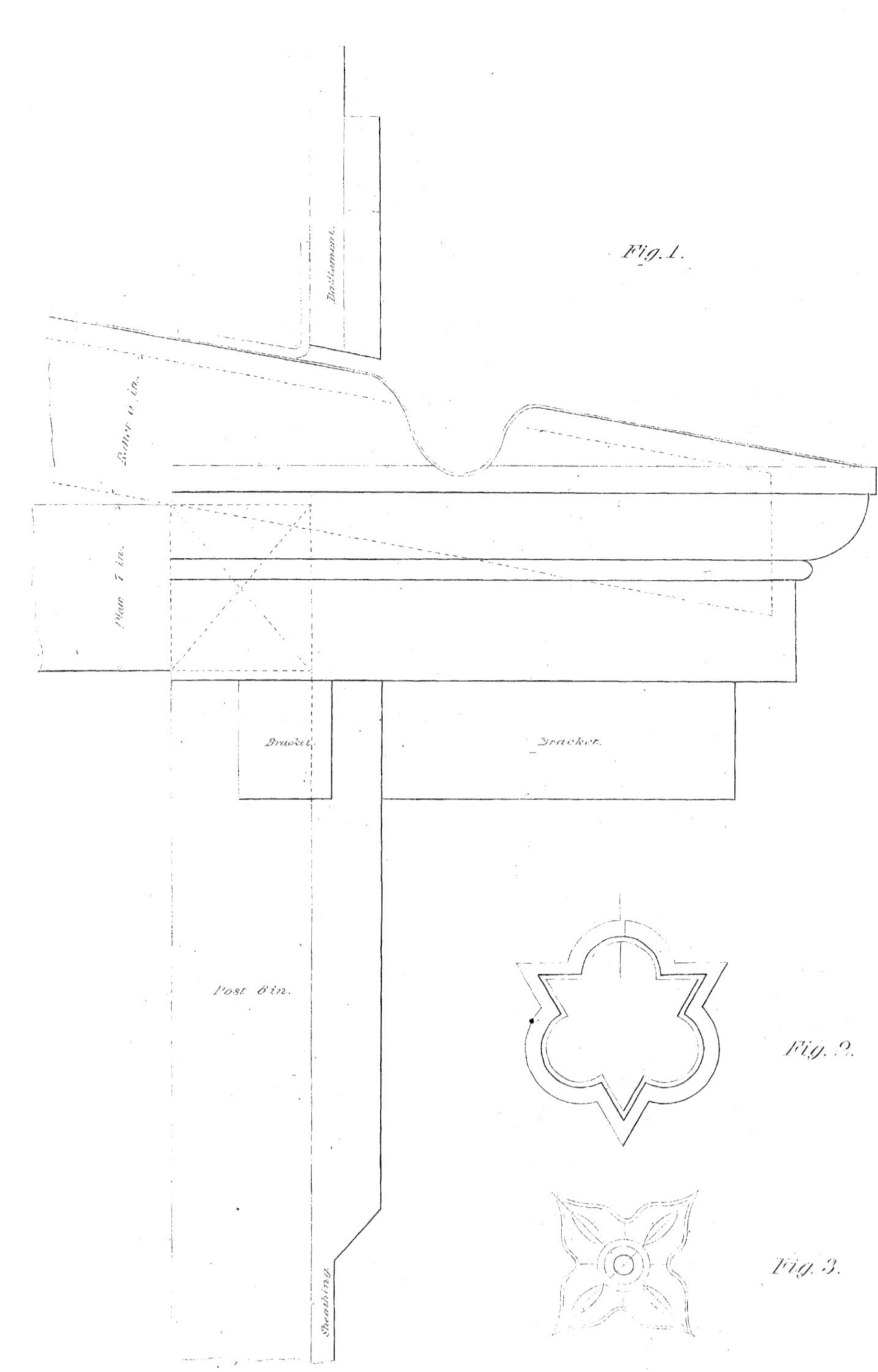

Fig. 1.
Battlement.
Rafter 6 in.
Plate 7 in.
Bracket.
Bracket.
Post 6 in.
Sheathing.
Fig. 2.
Fig. 3.

DETAILS OF CORNICE.

Plate XXIII.

Fig. 1.—A representation of the cornice, &c.

It will be understood by examination. Drawn to a scale of 2 in. to a foot.

Fig. 2.—A triangular window seen in the front elevation. Scale, 1 in. to a foot.

Fig. 3.—An ornament, shown in the elevation near the triangular window; half size.

From the hall we also enter the parlor, (*e*), which has a door to the ante-room, or conservatory; also to the kitchen, (*f*).

If preferred, (*d*) may be made the parlor, and (*e*) the dining-room, and then a communication may be made with the kitchen, (*f*).

The kitchen door from the hall is finished on the staircase side in the same manner as the doors of the principal rooms. From the kitchen there is a coal-closet, (*g*), back kitchen or wash-room,. with a copper, (*h*), closet, (*k*), pantry, (L), and a store-closet, (*i*).

There are, if desired, two water-closets, (*m*, *m*), both under cover, — one entering from the porch, the other from the piazza.

Under the principal stairs is a flight of steps, (O), shut in by a door, descending to the cellar. Behind the wash-room, at (P), may be a yard, surrounded by a high fence, and covered with shrubbery, where may be the wood-house, privy, well, &c. &c.

No. 29.

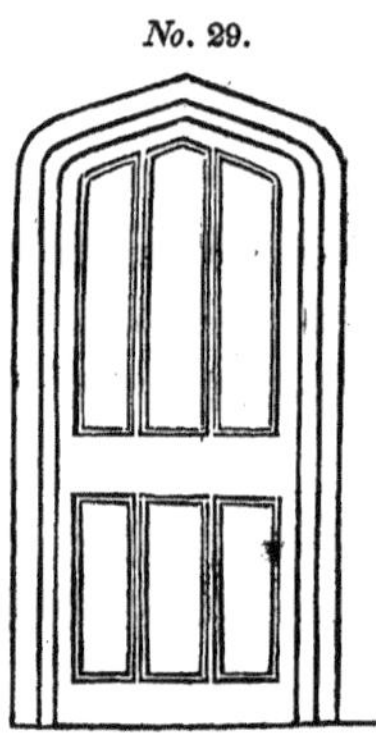

Fig. No. 29 shows an elevation of a door; it is surrounded on one side by splayed bricks, and is six feet high to the springing of the arch.

Fig. No. 30 shows an elevation of chimney-shafts, the base and cap of which are of stone, and the shaft and plinth rising from the roof of brickwork, or artificial stone, — the diameter of the flues nine inches.

No. 31 is a plan of the above elevation.

No. 32 is also a plan of the above elevation.

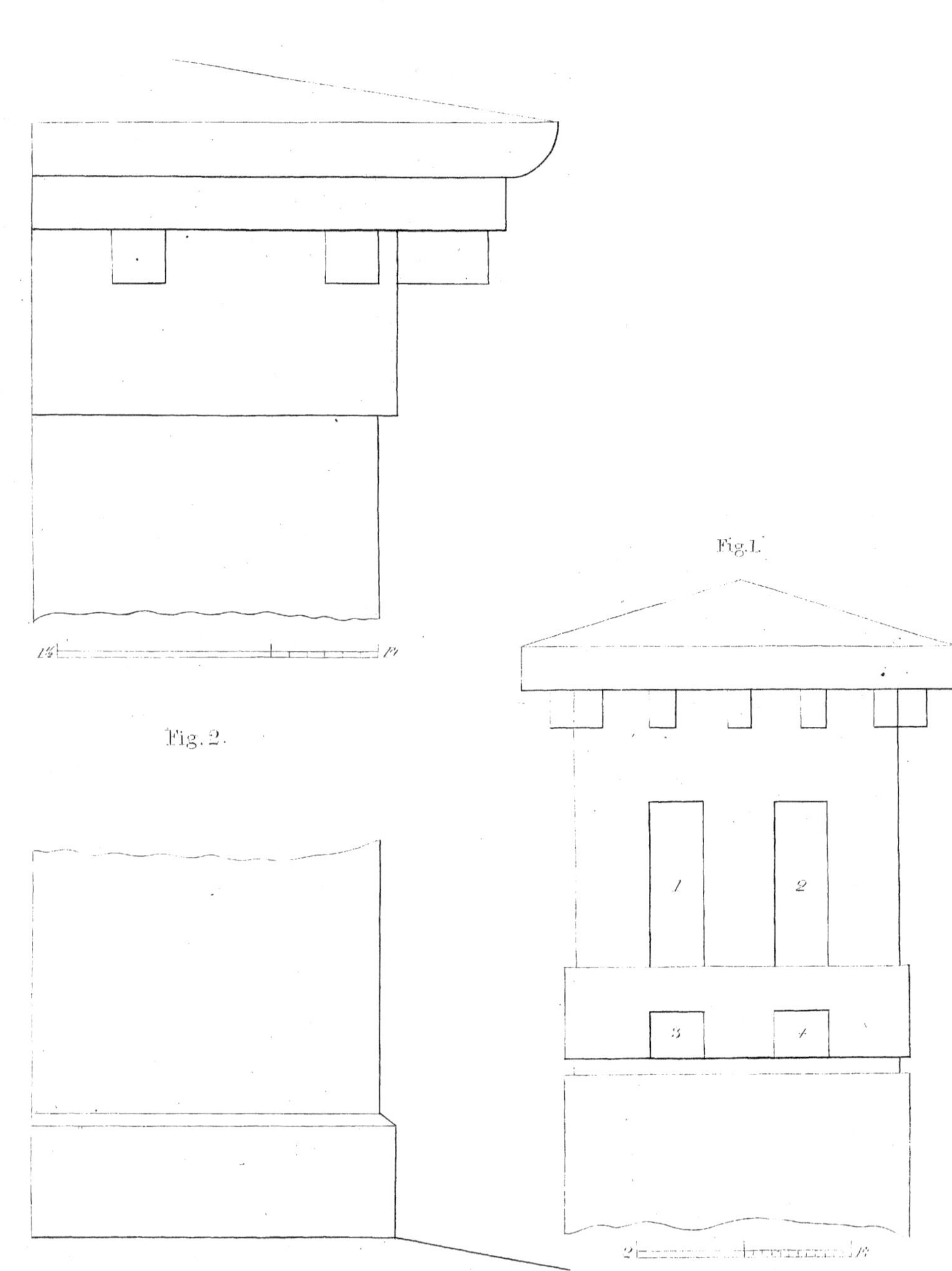

Fig. 2.

Wm Brown Archt

DETAILS.

PLATE XXIV.

THIS plate represents a design for a chimney, with a scale annexed. 1, 2, 3, 4, are openings for smoke. Also, a design for the external finish of the cupola. *Fig*. 1, chimney. *Fig*. 2, cupola.

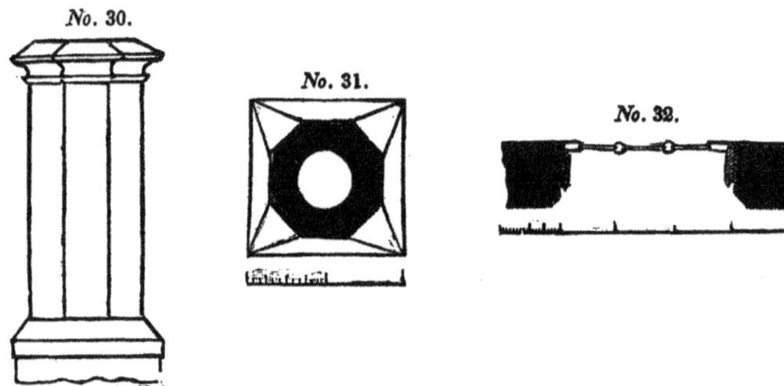

WOODEN EAVES-TROUGH, FOR COTTAGE ROOFS.

THIS finish to the eaves of a roof has now become very general for country-houses; and deservedly so, being the neatest, cheapest, and most durable of any, and adapted to the humblest cottage as well as to the elegant villa. This is made of the best clean, seasoned timber, with as few joints as possible, with mitred joints at the angles. It is fixed perfectly level, the fall being within itself, which is obtained by hollowing out the middle, beginning at (*o*, *c*), in No. 33, the highest part of the fall, and proceeding gradually deeper to (*z*), the lowest; thus a trough of this description may be fixed along a front of forty or fifty feet in length, the fall being given from the centre to the right and left. It requires no lining, but a good thorough painting, which should be repeated every three or four years. A large moulding being wrought on the front, it is thus made to represent the crowning member of a cornice.

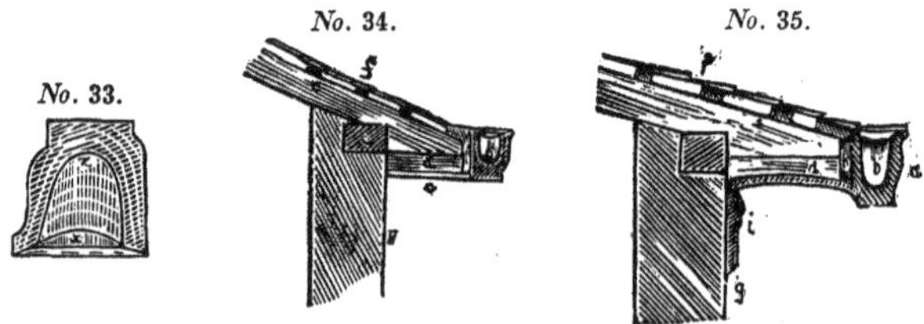

No. 34 represents the application of it to a cottage, where (*a*) is the moulded front of the eaves-trongh, (*b*) the hollow, (*c*) the plastered soffit, (*d*) bearer, (*e*) rafter, (*f*) slating, (*g*) front wall of house, (*h*) fascia, (*o*) wall-plate.

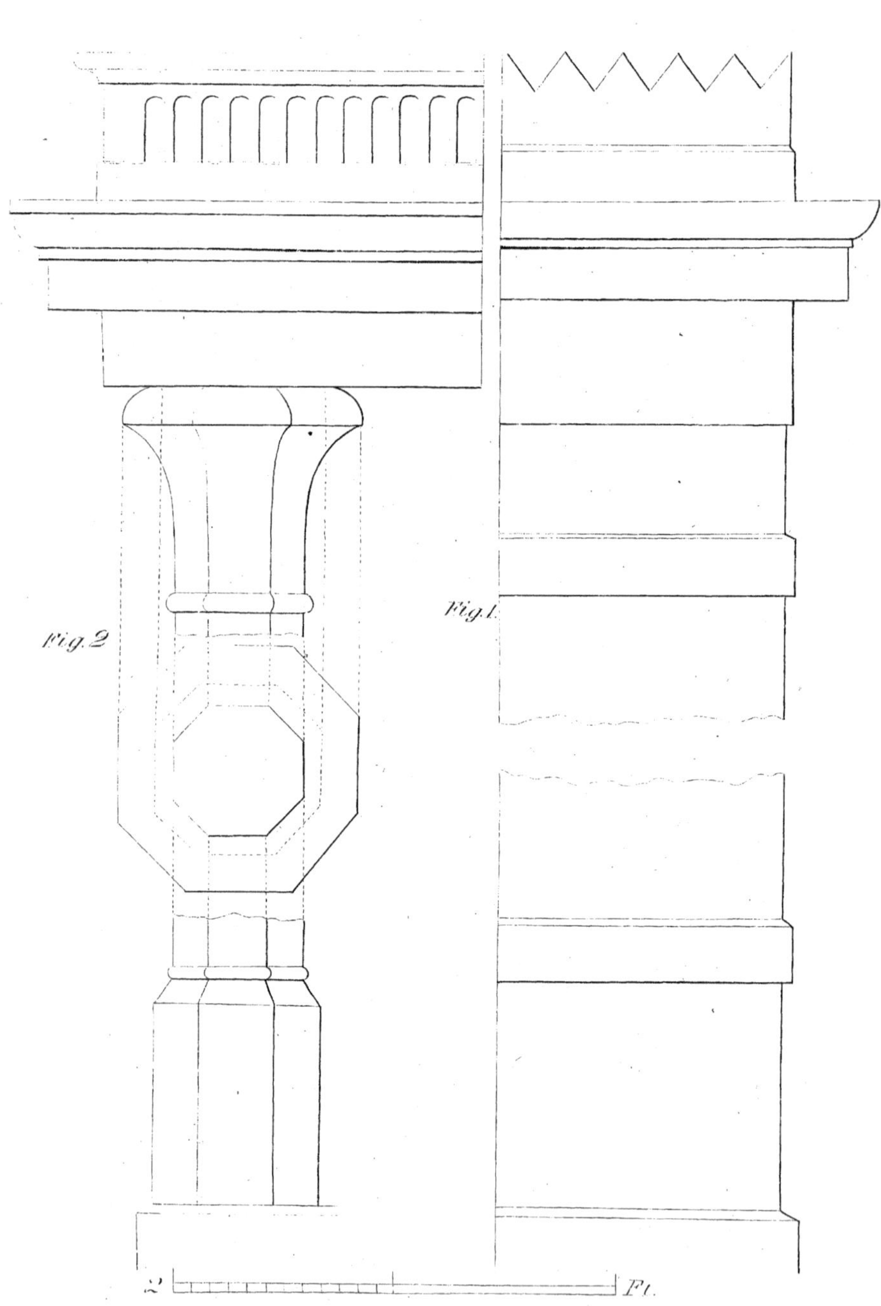
Fig. 2
Fig. 1.
2
Ft.

DETAILS OF PORTICO AND ORIEL WINDOW.

PLATE XXV.

ON this plate are two designs, which will be readily understood without any explanation.

Fig. 1, Oriel Window. *Fig*. 2, Portico.

No. 35, the same, with a higher style of finish. The same letters of reference answer. In addition, (*i*) shows a lead moulding and fascia in cement, and the plancier, (*c*), is curved. It may be finished in a still more elaborate style, with dentils or cantilevers, if required.

CAST-IRON GUTTERS TO ROOFS,

As a substitute for leaden ones, are found economical and effective. No. 36 represent a section of a gutter between two roofs, in which (*a*, *a*) shows the gutter, with a flange, (*b*, *b*), for joining the different pieces together; (*c*, *c*) the slates; (*d*, *d*) the rafters; and (*e*) the gutter rafter. All the care that this requires, in slating or shingling, is, to bring the upper edge of the lower course of slates or shingles to a level.

No. 36.

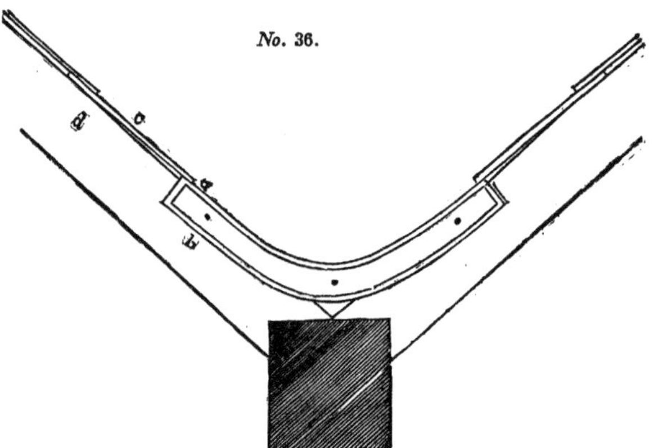

DES. I.

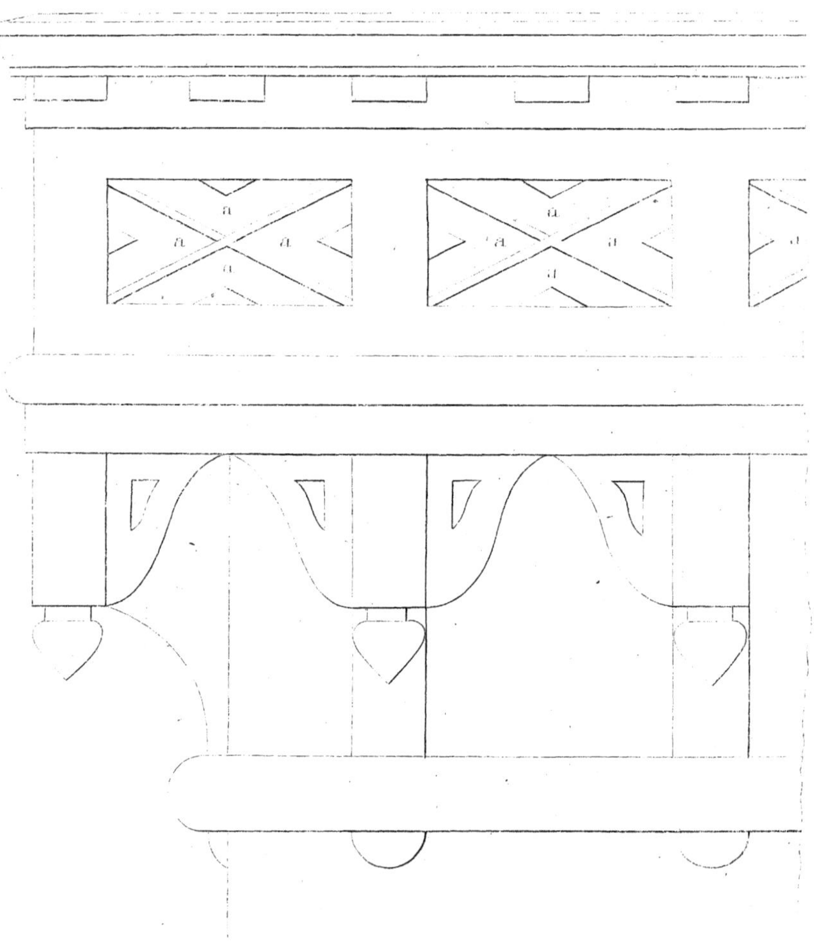

DETAILS.

PLATE XXVI.

THIS is a representation of the ornamental parapet-railing, over the porch of the front entrance. Scale, 2 inches to a foot; *a*, *a*, *a*, *a*, are openings.

No. 37.

THE TUDOR STYLE.

THE above elevation represents a cottage in the Tudor style, which fashion of architecture, so prevalent in the time of the Tudors, and called by that name, has been revived, to considerable extent, in cottage building, with very pleasing effect.

No. 38 represents the ground-plan for a flower-garden.

No. 38.

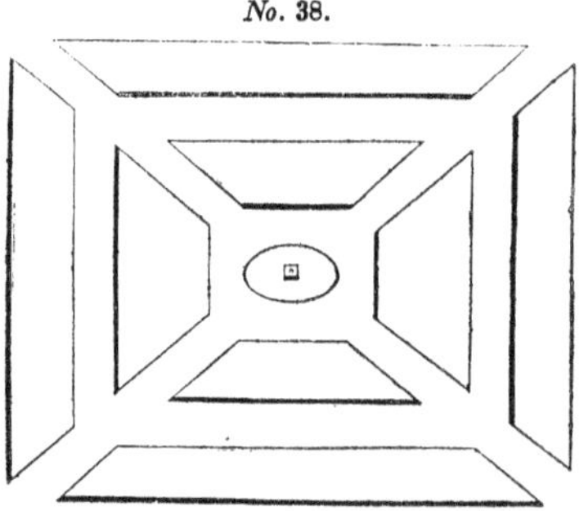

DETAILS OF DOOR AND WINDOW.

Plate XXVII.

This plate will be understood by measurement, and reference to the figures.

Fig. 1. *a*, stud; *b*, window weight; *c*, section of window sash; *d*, architrave; *e*, plastering; *f*, sheathing.

Fig. 2, is a section of an inside door and its finish; *a*, the architrave; *b*, jamb; *c*, door-stile; *d*, panel; *e e*, stud; *h*, plastering; and *i*, ground.

No. 39.

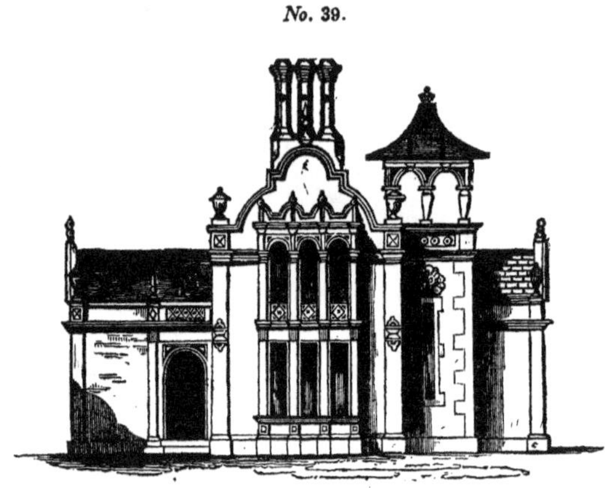

A COTTAGE IN THE ELIZABETHAN STYLE,

Is shown in the elevation No. 39.

The ground-plan, No. 40, shows a porch (*a*), hall (*b*), sitting-room (*c*), staircase (*d*), parlor (*e*), kitchen (*f*), bed-room (*g*), china closet (*h*), back entrance (*i*).

No. 40.

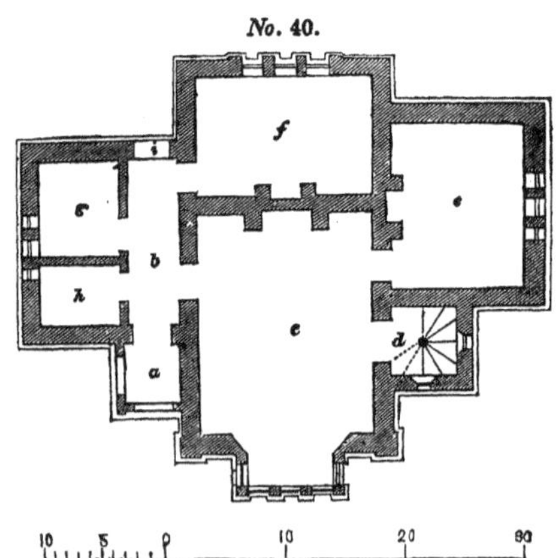

Fig. 1.

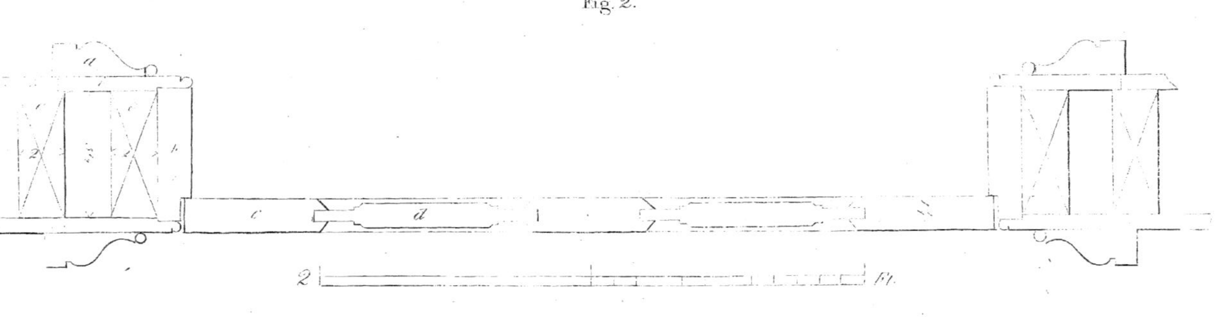

Fig. 2.

DES. I.

DETAILS OF DOOR AND FINISH.

Plate XXVIII.

A, an elevation of an inside door, with its finish and scroll ornament over the top. *B*, cornice and architrave, half size; *C*, cut-bead to ornament the architrave; *D*, base, half size.

No. 41.

VILLA IN THE ITALIAN STYLE.

THIS beautiful villa, the residence of Thomas A. Clark, Esq., of Worcester, Mass., has just been completed, from the designs and under the superintendence of the author.

This building is very much admired for chasteness and beauty, as well as its convenience. It is built of wood, with the roof covered with tin. The principal story is eleven feet in the clear; the chambers, ten feet in the clear; parlor, twenty-three feet six inches by fifteen feet, with the ceiling panelled, and moulded with an enriched moulding, with two beautiful centrepieces; hall, twenty-three feet six inches by eight, with front stairs leading to the second story; sitting-room, fifteen feet by fifteen; dining-room, fifteen feet by fifteen feet; kitchen, fifteen feet six inches by thirteen feet six inches; pantry, nine by eight feet; china closet, nine by five feet; wash-room, ten by fourteen feet; wood-room, ten by eight feet. The kitchen is fitted up with cooking-ranges; marble mantels in parlor, sitting and dining rooms; and a large-sized furnace in the cellar, for heating the house. All the doors grained in imitation of black walnut. Estimate the cost of this house to not vary much from $6000.

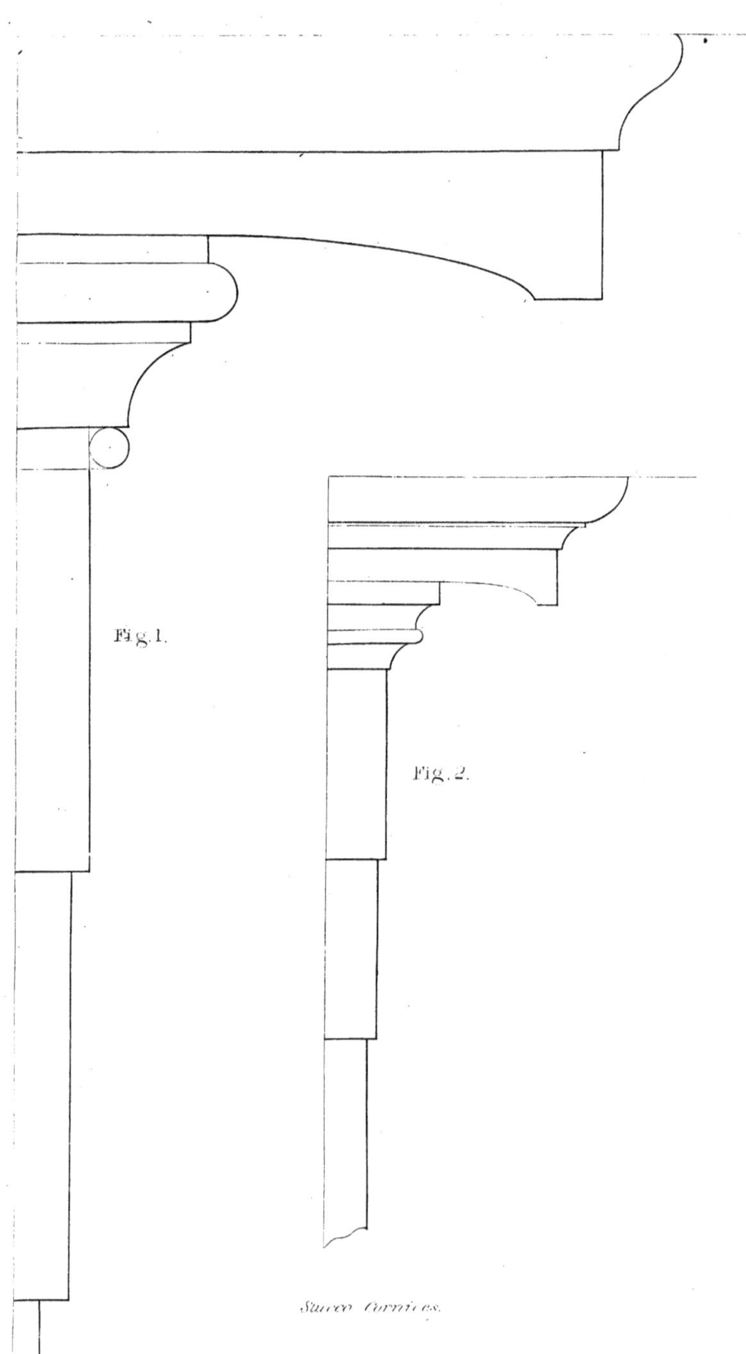

Stucco Cornices.

STUCCO CORNICES.

Plate XXIX.

On this plate are two designs for stucco cornices.

Fig. 1, is designed for the drawing-room and hall; half the real size.

Fig. 2, is designed for the parlor, library, and dining-room; one *quarter* the real size.

No. 42.

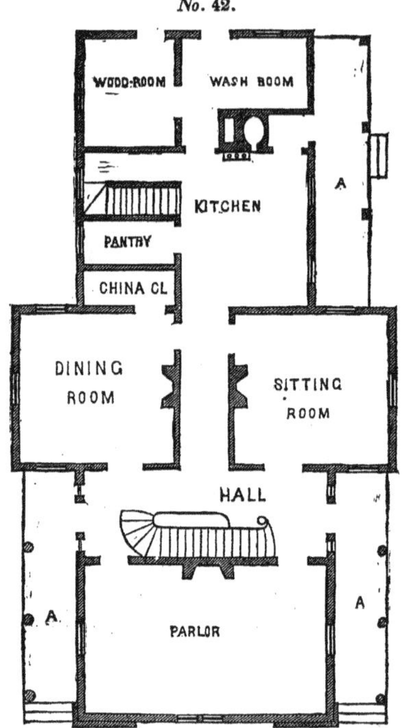

No. 42 shows the ground-plan to the front elevation, No. 41. No. 43 represents an elegant design for an arbor.

No. 43.

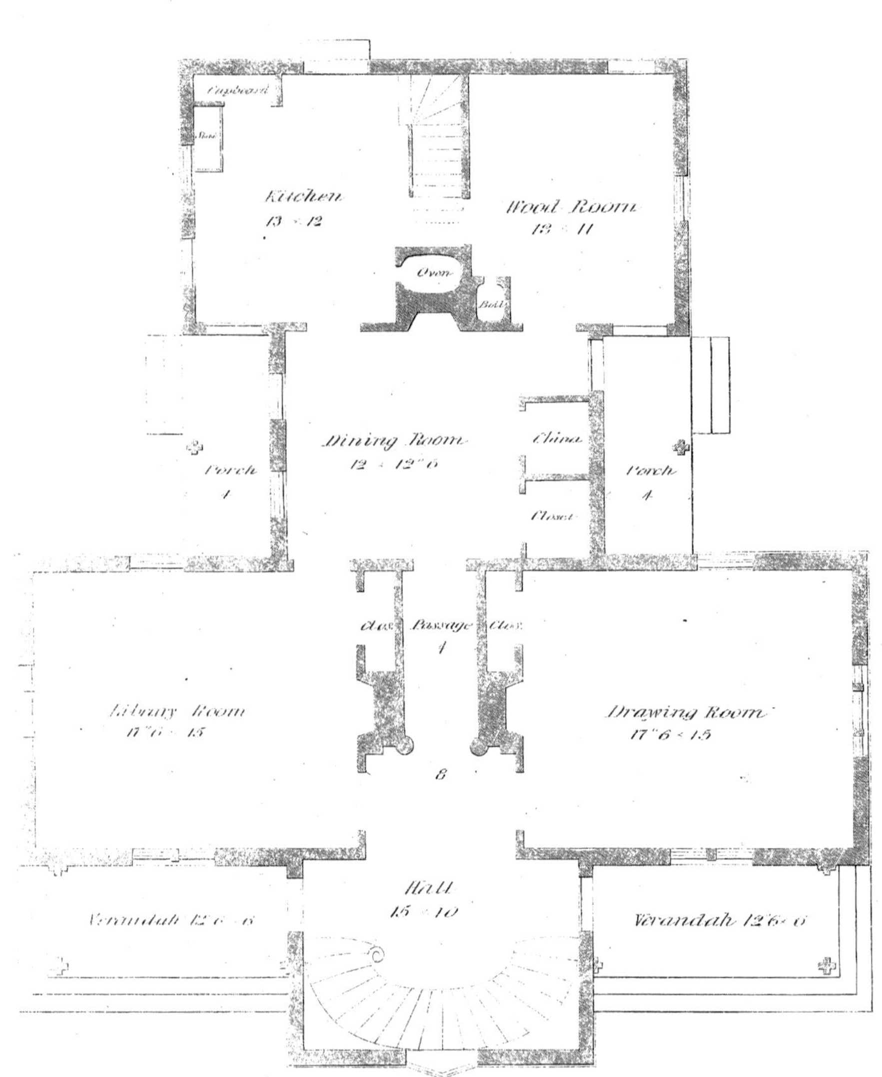
Cupboard
Kitchen
13 × 12
Wood Room
13 × 11
Oven
Boil
Dining Room
12 × 12"6
China
Closet
Porch
4
Porch
4
Clos.
Passage
4
Clos.
Library Room
17"6 × 15
Drawing Room
17"6 × 15
8
Hall
15 × 10
Verandah 12'6 × 6
Verandah 12'6 × 6

PLAN OF A COTTAGE HOUSE.

Plate XXX.

This plate represents the ground plan of a house in the cottage style. The back part, as far as the dining-room extends, is to be two stories high. The rest, or kitchen and wood-room, *one* story high; the cornice of which is to continue over the porches on each side of the dining-room. The front entrance is from the veranda on each side of the hall, as will be perceived.

No. 44.

GOTHIC VILLA.

THE elevation is shown in the above. The intention of this design is to show an ornamental style of architecture, which may be executed in a substantial manner at comparatively small cost.

FRONT ELEVATION.

Plate XXXI.

We here present the front elevation of a cottage house, drawn to a scale of one eighth of an inch to a foot. In all the designs the same scale is used, unless otherwise shown.

No. 45.

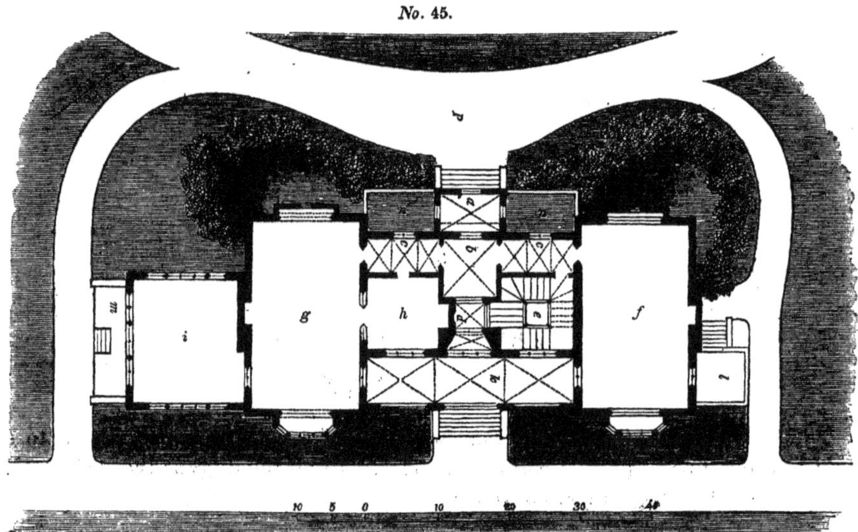

No. 45 represents the ground-plan to the preceding elevation. (*a*) is the porch, (*b*) the hall, (*c*, *c*) corridor, (*d*) lobby to the staircase, (*e*) staircase, (*f*) sitting-room, (*g*) parlor, (*h*) library, (*i*) conservatory, (*k*) arcade, (*l*) landing and steps down to the grounds, (*m*) landing, or terrace, and steps to the grounds from the conservatory, (*n*, *n*) areas, (*o*, *o*) sunk or sloped ground to give light and ventilation to the basement, and (*p*) approach road.

To the entrance of every house a porch is not only a luxury, but is necessary to protect the house from cold, and to form a suitable shelter in inclement weather. The entrance archway of this porch, (*a*), should be the largest opening in this front, and it should be conspicuously decorated, in order that it may at once mark the principal entrance.

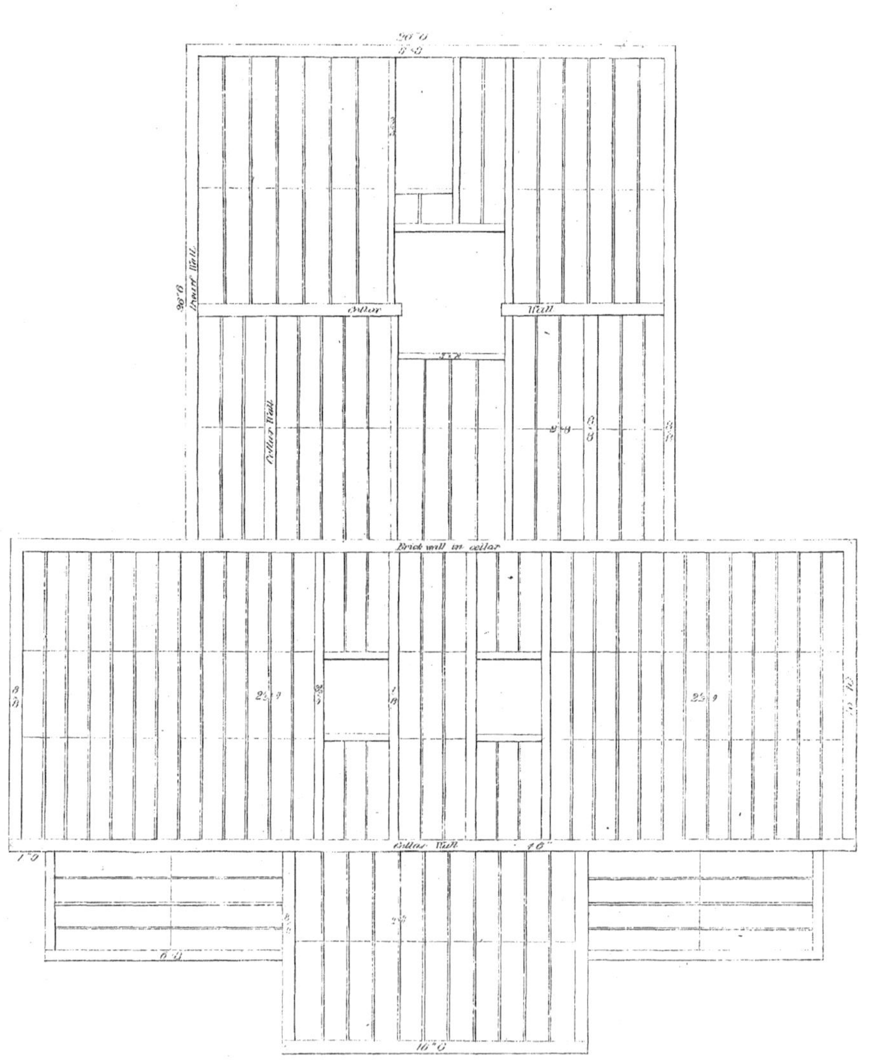
20'0
Board Wall
Cellar
Wall
Cellar Wall
Brick wall in cellar
23'9
23'9
Cellar Wall
16'0

FRAMING.

Plate XXXII.

Represents the first-floor framing. This needs no particular explanation. The sizes of the timbers are marked, &c.

BUEL'S BARN.

No. 46.

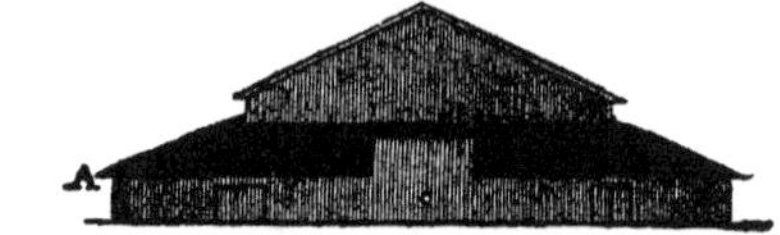

No. 46 (A) represents the end view.

No. 47.

No. 47 (B) shows a side view.

No. 48.

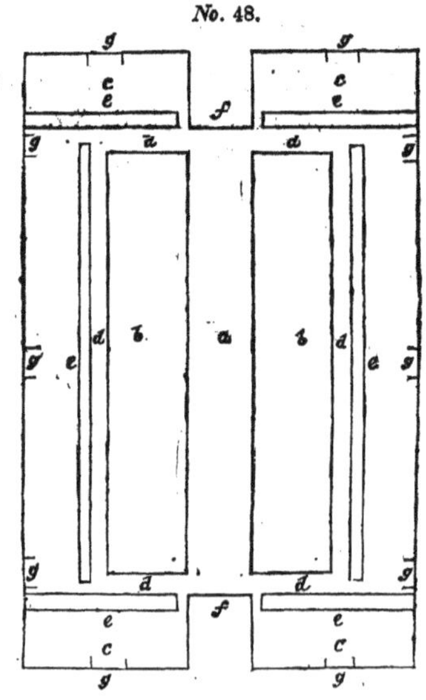

No. 48 is the ground-plan of a barn according to Buel's views. (*a*) is the barn floor, fourteen feet wide; (*b*, *b*) bays for hay and grain, eighteen feet

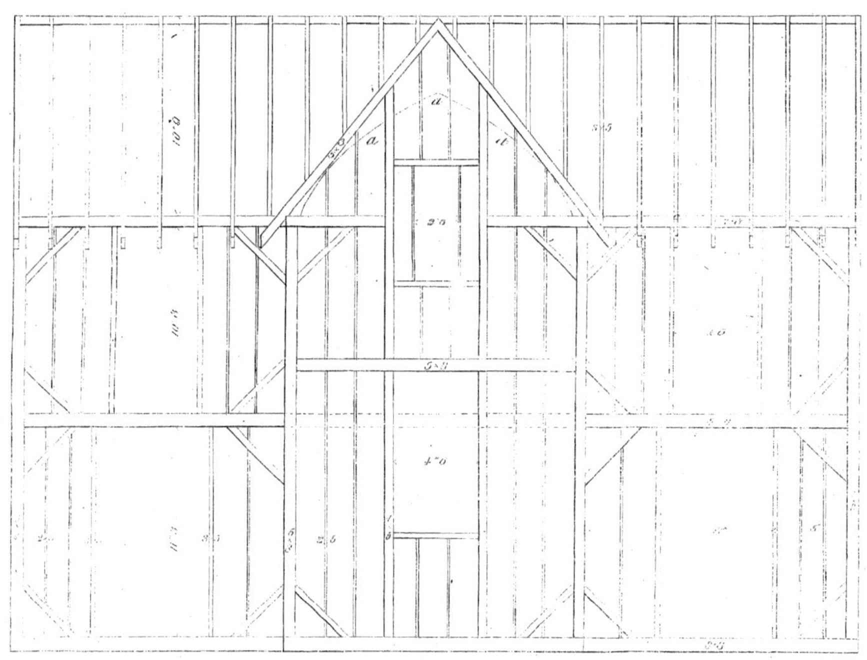

ELEVATION OF FRAME.

PLATE. XXXIII.

BY this plate is represented the elevation of frame for the cottage house. The front entry or hall to be arched, as shown at *a*, *a*, *a*.

The heights, openings, and sizes of timbers, are marked in feet and inches.

wide and ninety-two feet long; (*c, c*) stables for cattle and horses, thirteen feet wide in the clear; (*d, d*) passages to stable, four feet wide; (*e, e*) mangers for feeding, two and one half feet wide; (*f, f*) great doors, fourteen feet wide; (*g, g*) stable doors, five feet wide, double. Length of barn, one hundred feet; width, fifty feet; posts, eighteen feet; pitch of roof, twelve and one half feet; height of lean-to posts, seven feet; pitch of stable roof, eight feet; length of side lean-tos, one hundred feet; length of end lean-tos, thirty-eight feet. The barn is framed as if to stand alone, omitting the lower girt at the ends on each side of the large doors. The lean-tos are then framed on to the barn in the simplest manner, the passage being round the main body of the barn, excepting at the ends, where the passage is in the main barn, and the lean-tos there are only sixteen feet wide, and the manger is fitted up to the main barn. Only one passage is made to go into the shut stables at the ends. Stalls are made, seven and one half feet wide, and boarded between, and each ox or cow is tied next to the partition side of the stall, which prevents their getting together, and saves room.

This barn will hold two hundred tons of hay. Granaries can be partitioned off from the bays or stables, as may be convenient. On this model barns of any size may be built.

No. 49.

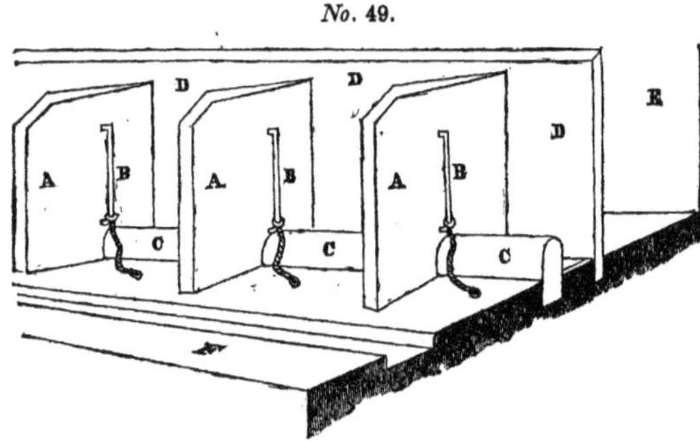

No. 49 shows a plan for the internal arrangement of cattle-sheds, &c., a movable ring and chain being used for confining the animals. A, A, A, partitions between the animals; B, B, B, the upright iron rods or posts to which are fixed the rings and chains; C, C, C, the raised edges of the manger in front; D, D, D, the partition; E, the passage in front; and F, that behind the animals.

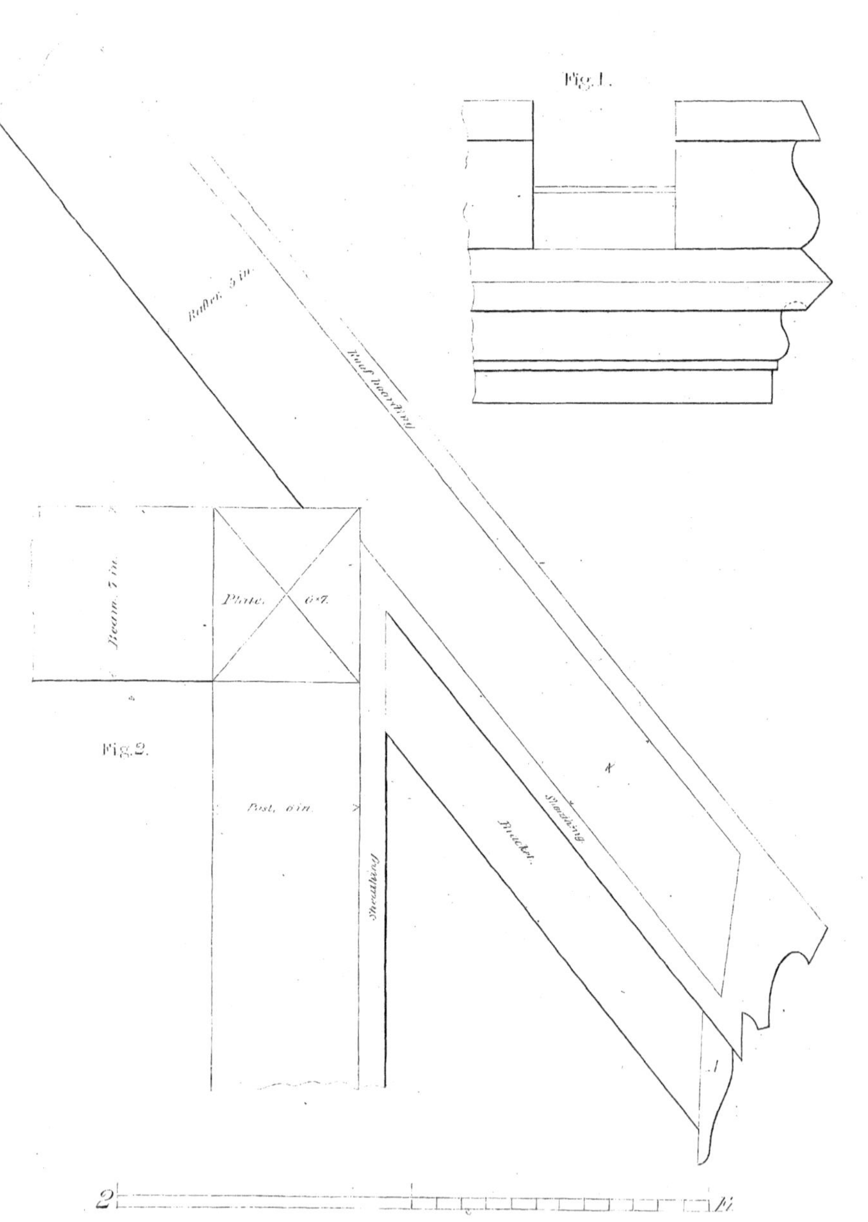
Fig. 1.
Rafter, 5 in.
Plate.
6×7.
Beam, 7 in.
Fig. 2.
Post, 6 in.
Sheathing
Bracket.
2
Ft.

DETAILS.

PLATE XXXIV.

ON this plate are shown two designs for outside finish.

Fig. 1.—Cornice and battlement of the portico.

Fig. 2.—Main cornice, &c.

A, an ornament which covers the ends of the bracket, as seen in the front elevation.

No. 50.

MODEL OF THE WASHINGTON BARN.

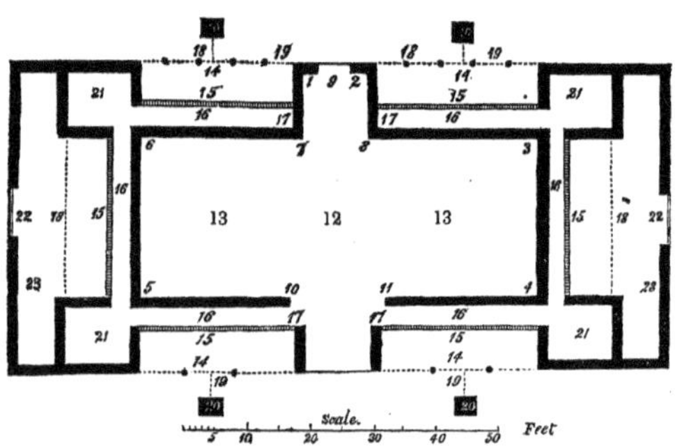

THE above is a plan of the barn structure sketched by Arthur Young for General Washington.

Figures 1, 2, 3, 4, 5, 6, represent the barn; 1, 2, 7, 8, the porch of do., with a small door at 9; 10, 11, the great doors; 12, the floor, which extends the space of 1, 2, 10, 11; 13, 13, bays; 14, 14, 14, 14, sheds; 15, 15, 15, 15, mangers; 16, 16, 16, 16, passages, between two and three feet wide; 17, 17, 17, 17, doors into the passage; 18, 18, 18, 18, principal posts on which the sheds rest; 19, 19, 19, 19, gutters of bricks sloped for conveying the urine of the cattle to 20, 20, 20, 20, cisterns; 21, 21, 21, 21, sheds for various purposes; 22, 22, two yards, with each a shed for shelter; 23, 23, enclosure; 1, 2, 8, 3, 4, 5, 6, 7, the main body of the barn, which rises from fourteen to twenty feet to the eaves, all the rest of the shed being placed against it.

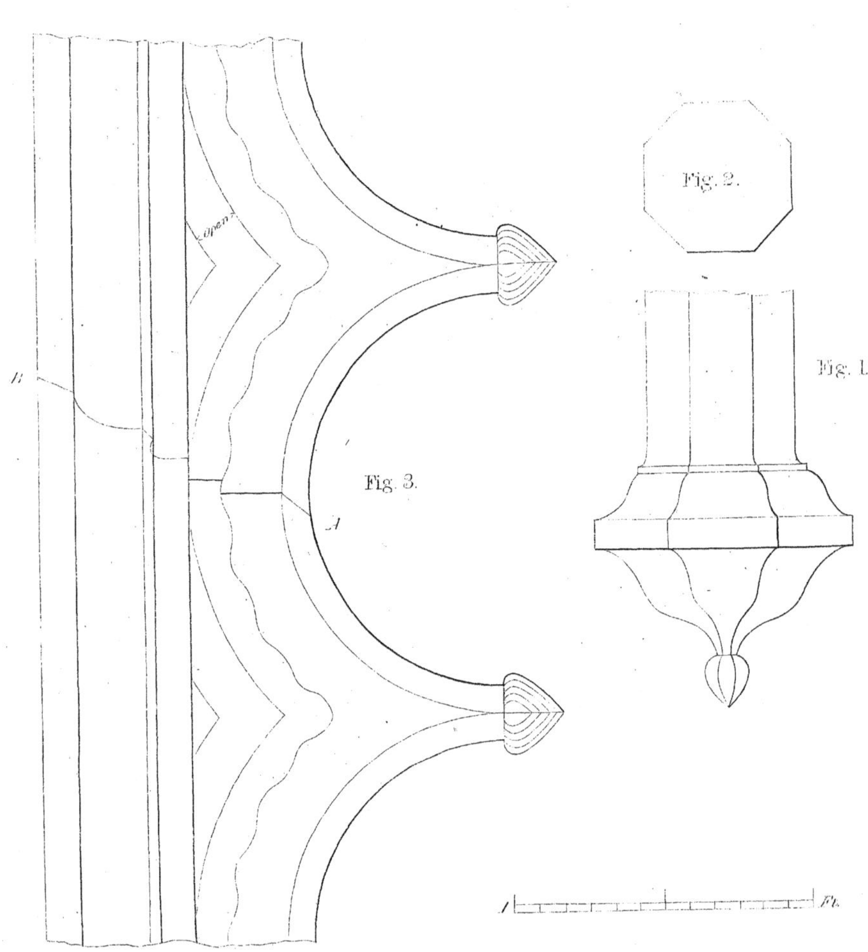

Wm. Brown. Archt.

W. H. Kimere Eng.

DETAILS.

Plate XXXV.

Fig. 1.—The pendant in the angle of the roof or pediment.

Fig. 2.—Section of the same.

Fig. 3.—Ornamented barge-board. From *A* to *B*, a section of the cornice and barge.

No. 51.

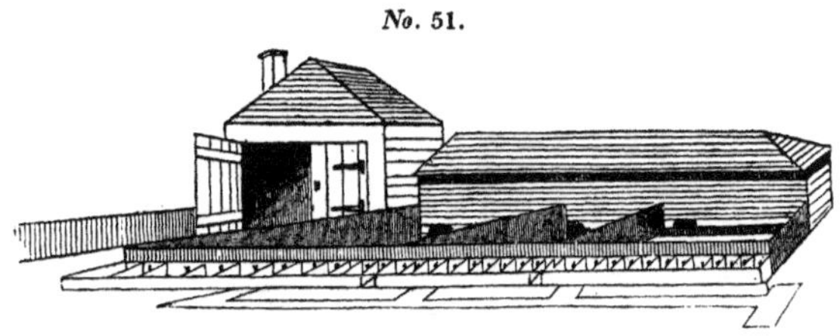

No. 51 gives a representation of a piggery, which should be raised upon a little declination, so as to allow the drainage of the urine, and divided into sties of between six and seven feet in width and fourteen or fifteen feet long, the back part of which should be covered with a low roof, and sufficiently large to allow a fatting hog to lie down conveniently. The uncovered part, which is used as a court for the animal to feed in, &c., should be boarded in front by a low paling, so as to admit of sun and air, and the trough placed in one corner. The building may be extended to any length, and if connected at one end with a boiling-house, and at the other with a cess-pool, into which the drains are emptied, the elevation of the whole will present the appearance as indicated in No. 51.

No. 52.

No. 52 shows an apartment for boiling or steaming food, apparatus necessary, and mode of proceeding. Any kind of wooden box or barrel will answer for this purpose. The steam is to be conveyed in a pipe to the lower part of the vessel, which should have a sliding board at the bottom.

The apparatus consists of a furnace and iron boiler, A, furnished with a safety-valve. It is supplied from a cistern, B, placed at the height of five or

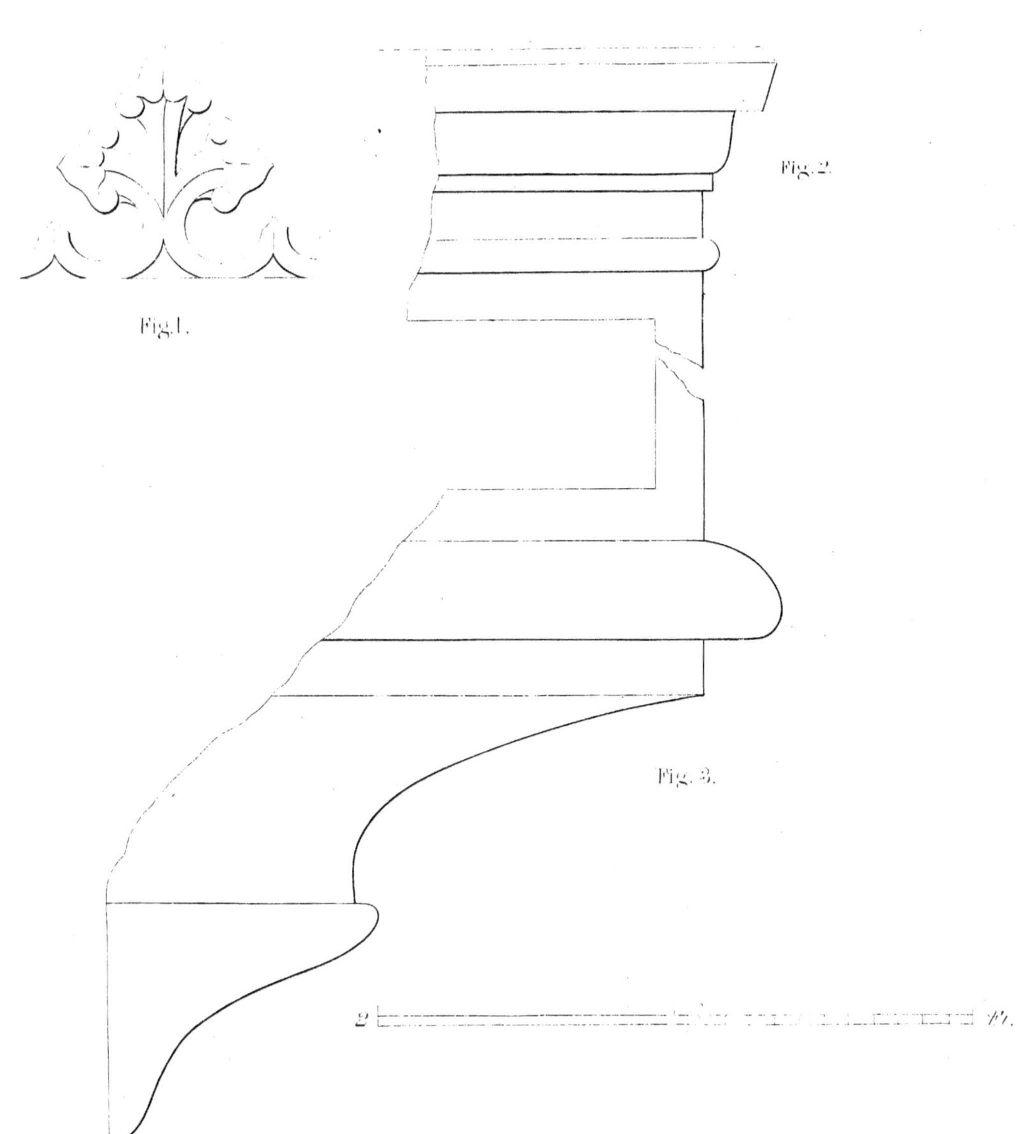
Fig. 1.
Fig. 2.
Fig. 3.
2
Ft.

DETAILS.

Plate XXXVI.

Fig. 1.—The ornament surmounting the cornice of the Oriel window seen in the front elevation, half size.

Fig. 2.—The cornice of the Oriel window.

Fig. 3.—The pedestal or base of the same.

six feet above it. When filled, the boiler regulates its supply of water by means of a float inside, attached to the valve in the cistern. Two casks, C and D, are intended to hold the potatoes, or other matter to be steamed,—the steam being conducted to these, from the boiler, by a pipe branching off to each by stop-cocks.

No. 53.

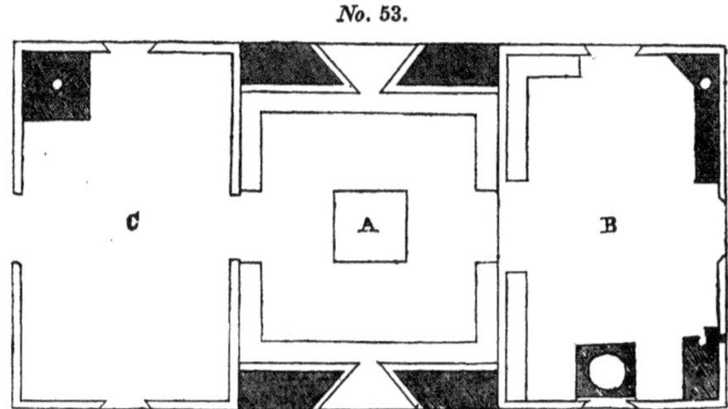

No. 53, as above, represents a plan for a dairy-house, the roof of which should be of a high conical form, or span roof, rising from the centre, and projecting downwards broadly over the sides, to shade the body of the house. (A) represents the milk-room, with broad shelves around the sides, and in the middle a table for preparing the butter. The windows are closed with lattices covered with gauze wire. (B) the churning-room, with boiler in one corner, and, on sides, frames for cheese-presses, and vessels for holding the whey, and pipes for conveying it to a cistern outside. (C) the wash-house, for cleansing and care of the utensils; it therefore contains a furnace, with a cauldron for scalding the vessels, and a pump, communicating with a well. The outer door, or entrance, is here; and adjoining are placed stands, under the verandah formed by the projection of the roof, for exposing the wooden implements which may have been washed to be dried.

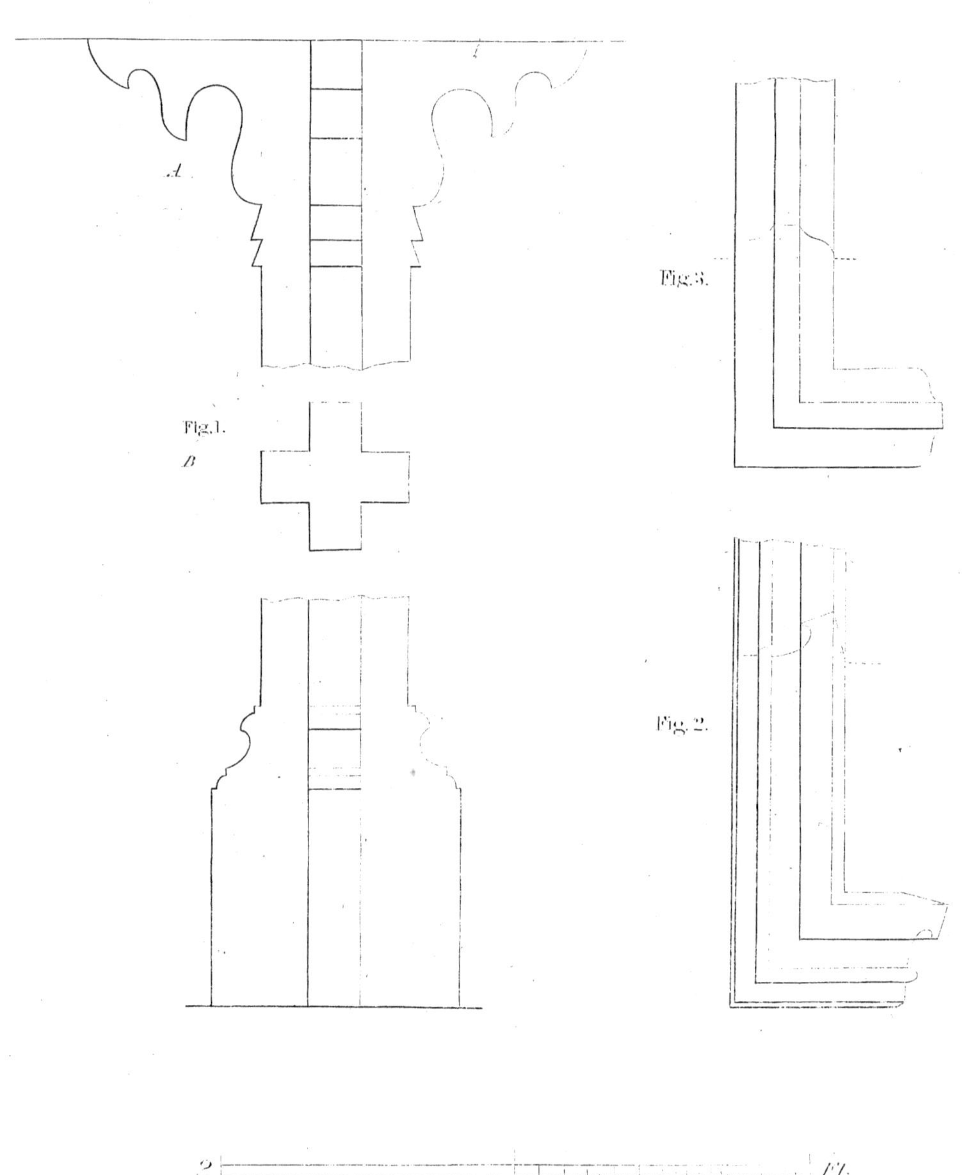

Brown Archt

DETAILS.

PLATE XXXVII.

Fig. 1.—Column of the portico in front. ***A***, bracketed capital ; ***B***, a section of the column ; *C*, base.

Figs. 2 and 3, are two examples of hoods for outside finishing of windows. (See elevation.)

No. 54.

MODEL OF A COMPLETE DAIRY.

The above front elevation represents a view of a complete dairy, which may form a part of the farmer's house, or be distinct from it.

No. 55.

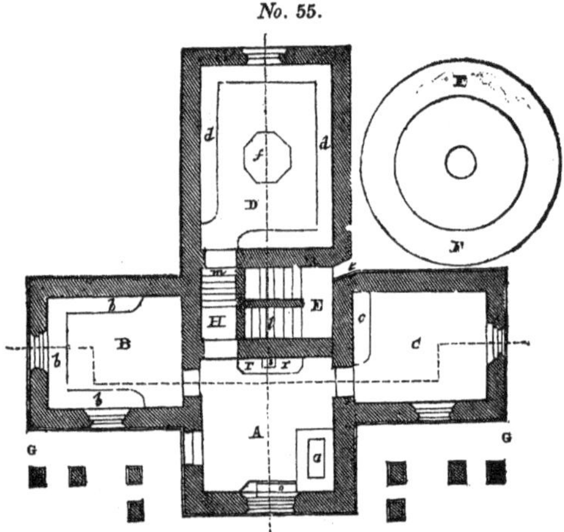

The ground-plan is shown in No. 55. (A) is the kitchen; (*a*), steam boiler; (*o*), sink in the window recess, in which the water can be heated by a steam pipe from the boiler; (*s*), small sink, communicating with the pigs' troughs, in which the whey and other refuse are thrown; (*r*, *r*), stone benches; (E), wood and coal cellar, with hatch, (*e*), by which the fuel is

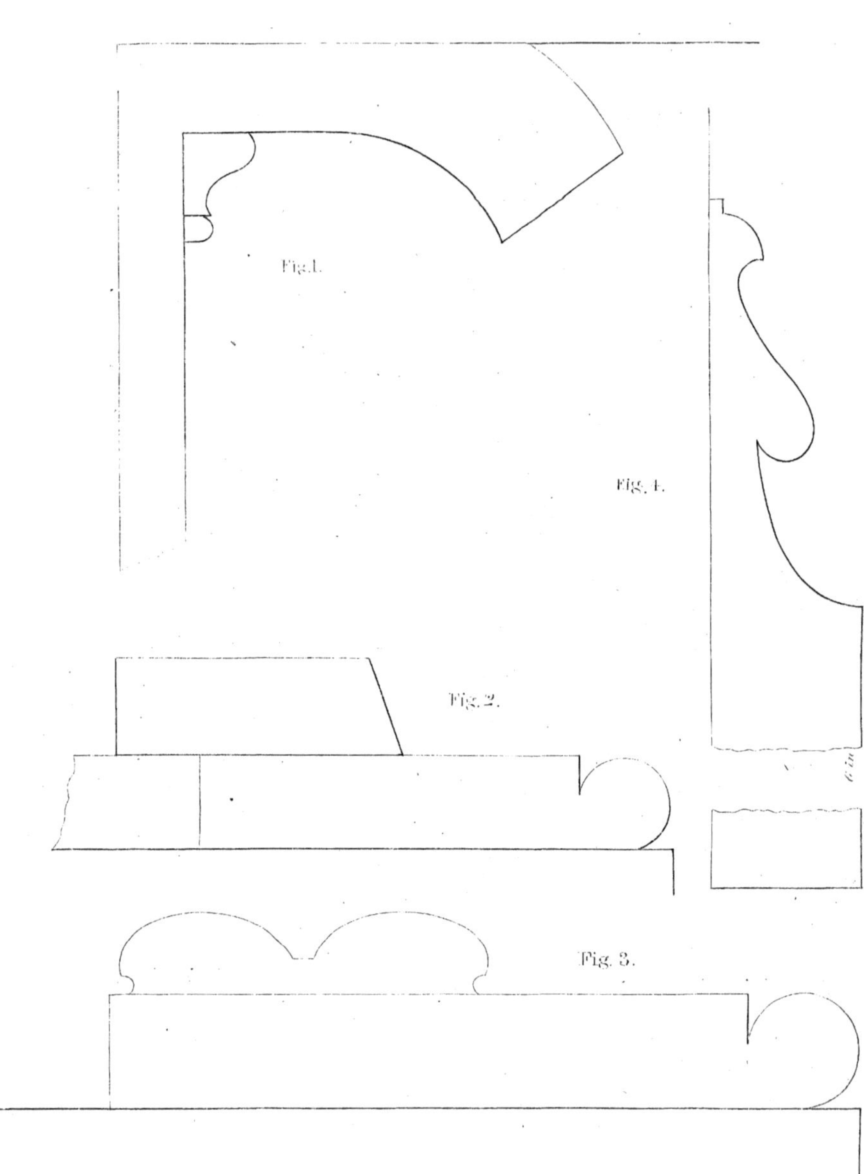
Fig. 1.
Fig. 4.
Fig. 2.
6 in
Fig. 3.

DETAILS.

PLATE XXXVIII.

Fig. 1.—Stucco cornice, half the real size.
Figs. 2 and 3.—Plans of architraves.
Fig. 4.—Base moulding.
Figs. 2, 3 and 4, are of full size.

thrown in; (C), churning-room; (*c*), stone bench for milk-vessels; (B), cheese-making room; (*b, b, b*), stone bench for utensils; (D), milk-room; (*d, d*), stone bench round the room, for milk-vessels; (*f*), table for preparing butter, with basin and fountain; (*g, g*), shed along the front of the building; (F, F), horse course for moving the churn; (H), passage; (*m*), stairs down to milk-room; (L), stairs to the upper part.

No. 56.

No. 56 shows a side elevation of the foregoing No. 54. In plan of the upper floor, represented in No. 57, (A) is the store-room; (B), store-room; (*b, b*), shelves; (*c*), landing of stairs; (D), upper landing; (E), cistern; (*e*), closet.

No. 57.

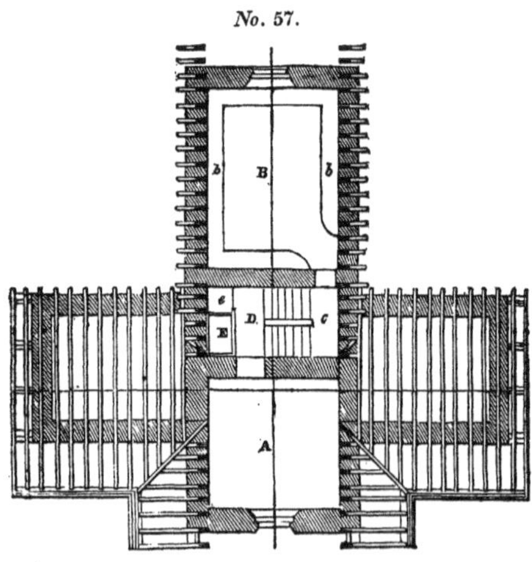

DES. II.

Wm. Brown, Arch.

W. B. Emory, Eng.

INSIDE DOOR.

PLATE XXXIX.

THIS plate shows an elevation of an inside door and finish, showing a section through the centre.

No. 58.

The above is a partial view of a beautiful cottage built for Wm. B. Lang, Esq., on the Highlands in Roxbury.

No. 59.

This is a view of a noble villa erected at Wyoming, on the borders of Spot Pond, near Medford, and late the residence of Wm. B. Lang, Esq.

No. 60.

The above is a plan of a castellated house.

DES. III.

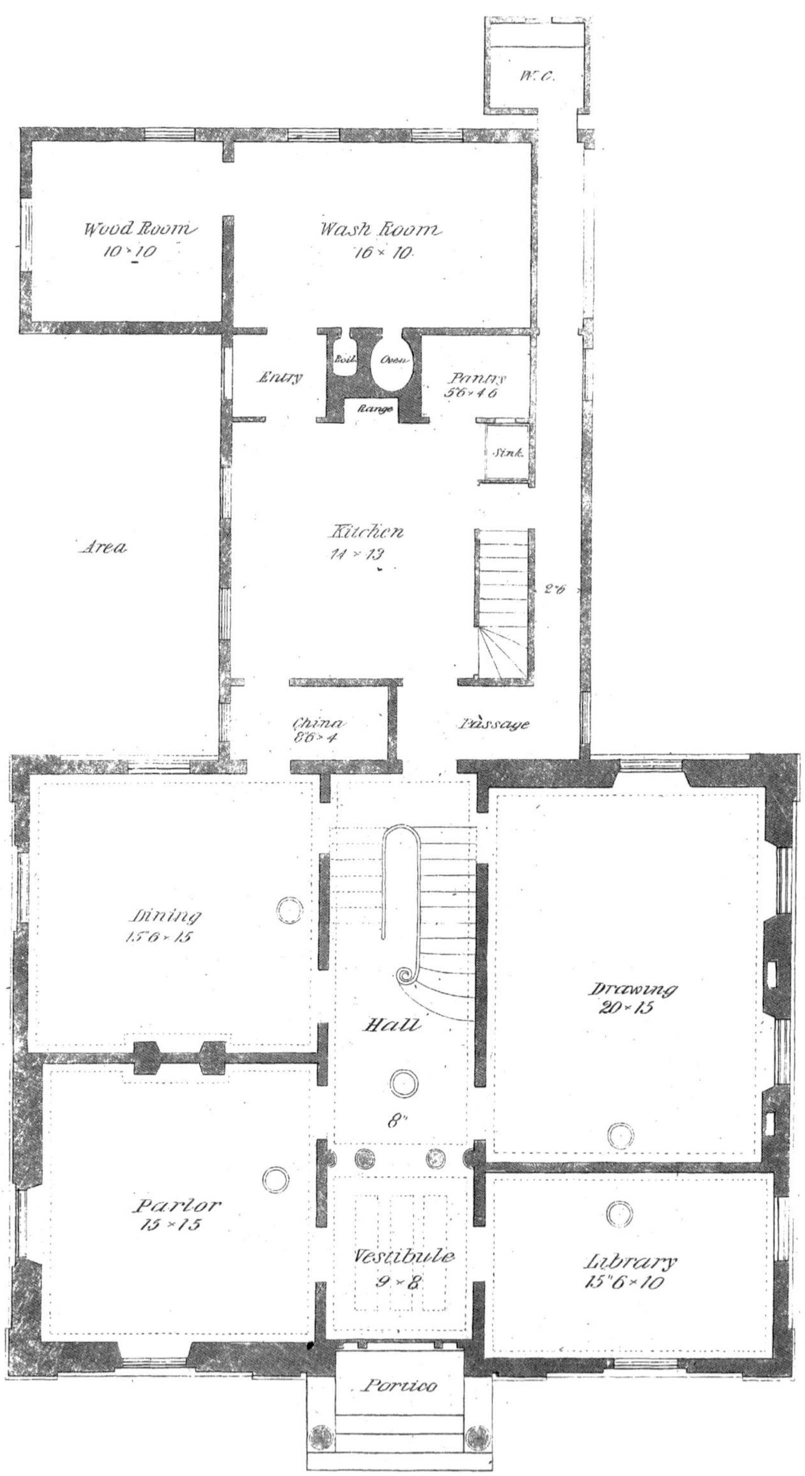

W. C.
Wood Room
10 × 10
Wash Room
16 × 10
Boil
Oven
Range
Entry
Pantry
5'6 × 4'6
Sink
Area
Kitchen
14 × 13
2'6
China
8'6 × 4
Passage
Dining
15'6 × 15
Hall
8"
Drawing
20 × 15
Parlor
15 × 15
Vestibule
9 × 8
Library
15"6 × 10
Portico

PLAN OF A GRECIAN HOUSE.

Plate XL.

This plate represents a ground plan of a house in the Grecian style. We consider this kind of house very economical, both in respect to expense and convenience. By an examination of the plate it will be under stood, as the sizes are marked, &c.

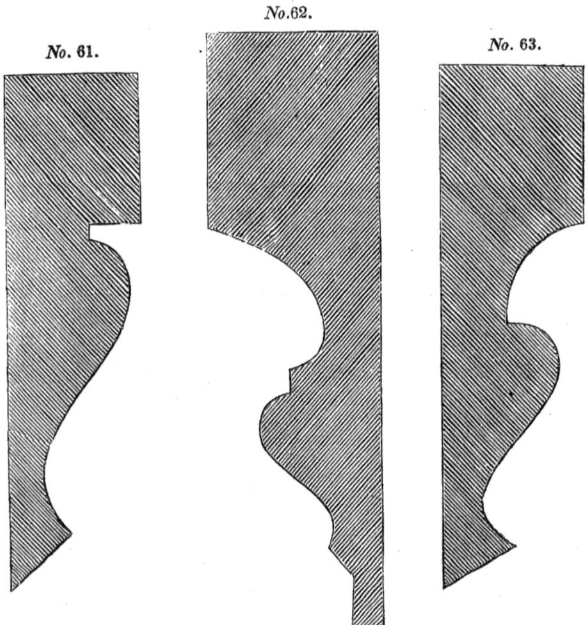

Nos. 61, 62, 63, 64, 65, 66, 67, exhibit seven designs for base, and architrave mouldings, full size, for practice.

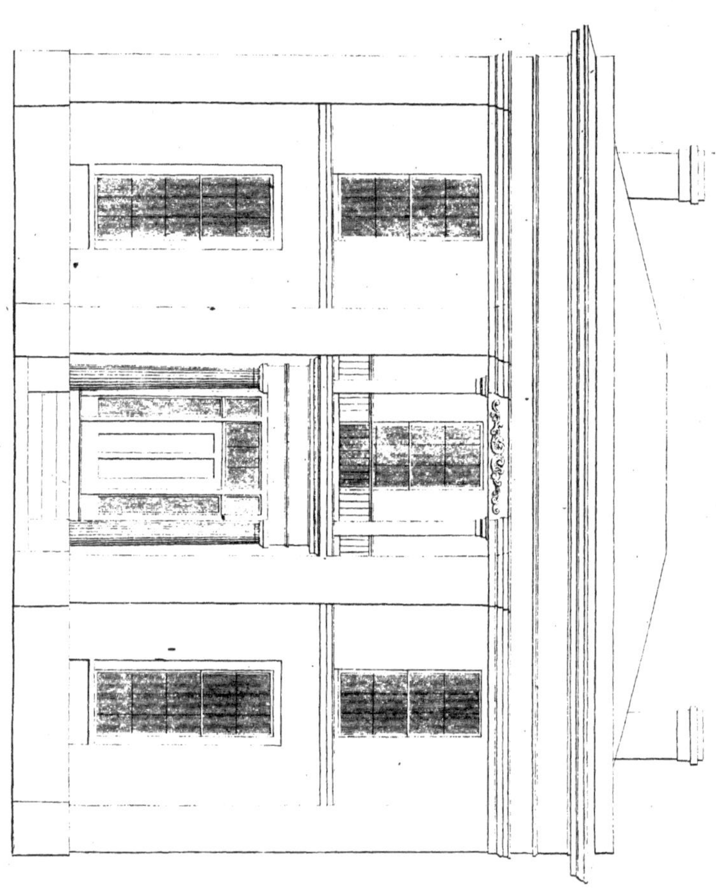

Wm. Brown, Archt.

FRONT ELEVATION.

Plate XLI.

This plate presents a front elevation of the Grecian house shown in the last sketch. It is a chaste, simple, and graceful design, and one, we think, which will meet the expectations of any gentleman who may see fit to adopt it in building.

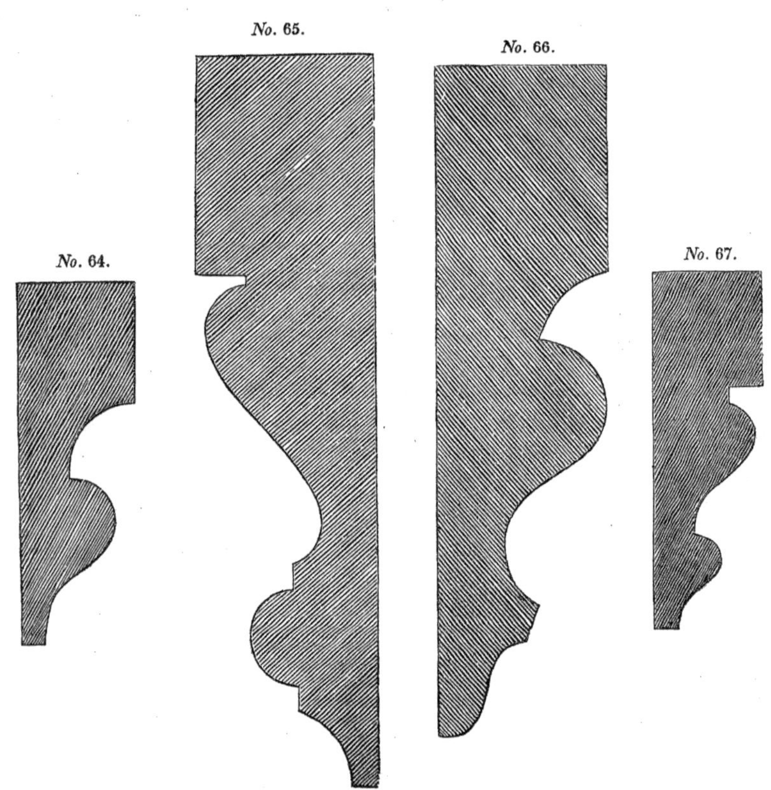
No. 64.
No. 65.
No. 66.
No. 67.

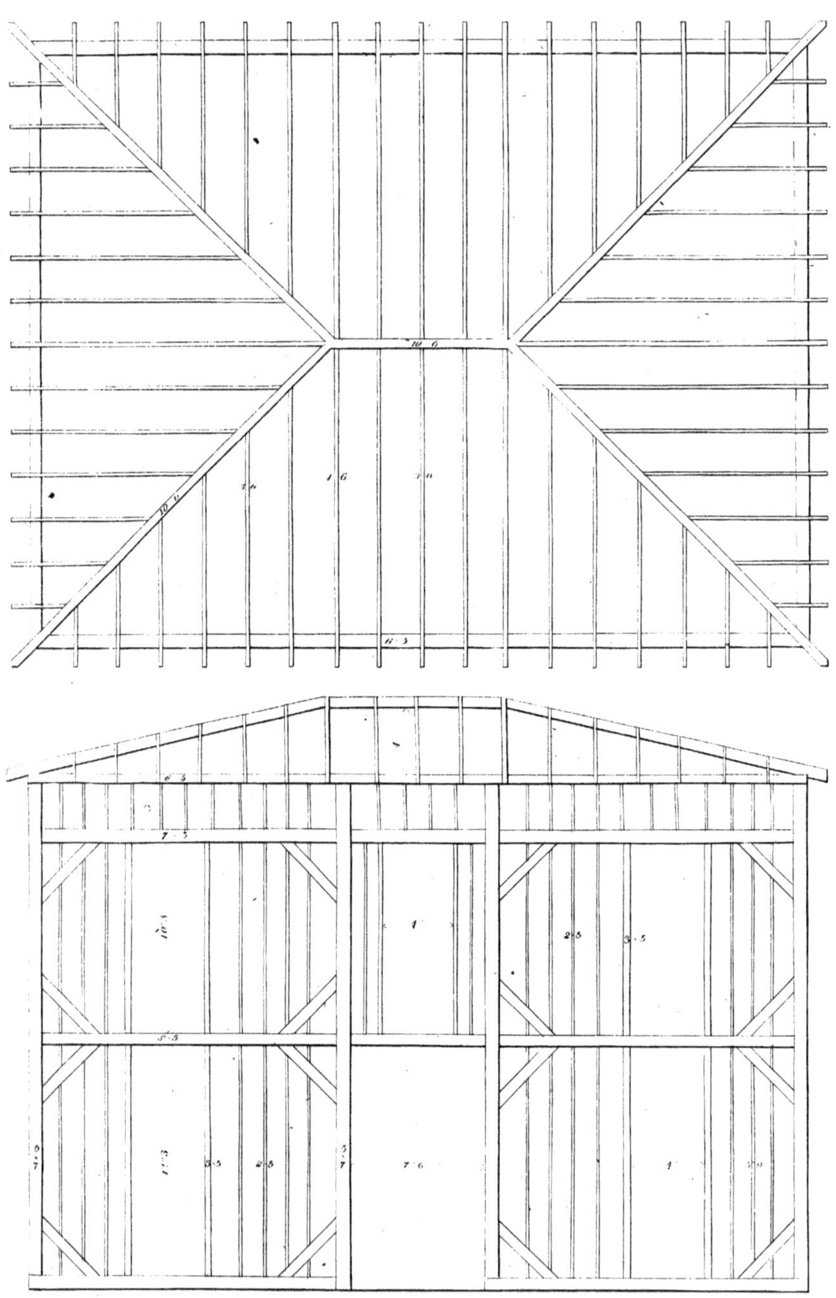

Wm. Brown, Arch't. W. B. Emery, Eng.

ELEVATION OF FRAME.

Plate XLII.

This plate shows an elevation of the framing and plan of the roof so plainly as to need no explanation. The sizes of the timbers, height, and spaces, are all marked, &c.

No. 68.

The front elevation, No. 68, as represented above, exhibits a modern and beautifully-constructed house, built for the Rev. Seth Sweetser, of Worcester, Mass., and designed by Mr. Elbridge Boyden.

No. 69 shows the end elevation of the same house.

No. 69.

PLT. XLII

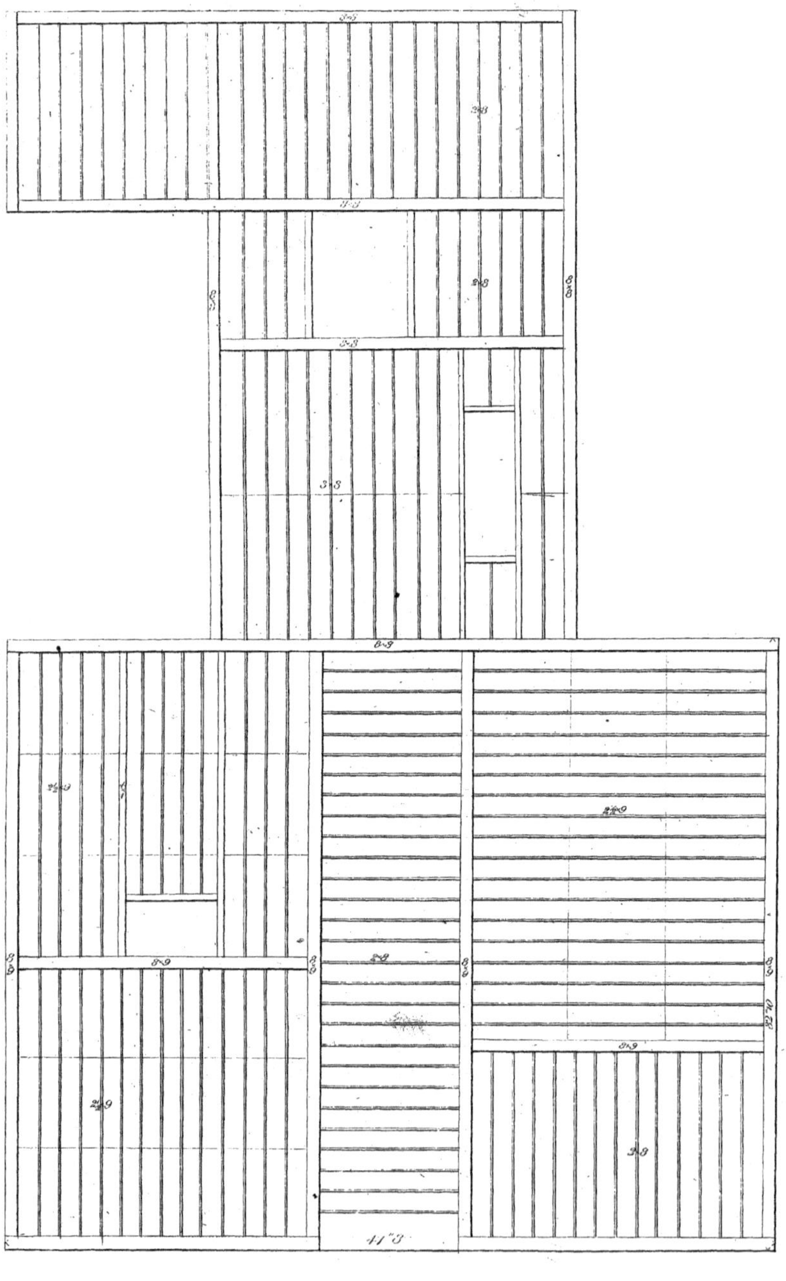

GROUND FLOOR FRAMING.

Plate XLIII.

This plate shows the frame for the ground floor of the Grecian house, with a proper arrangement of timbers, and their sizes marked, &c.

No. 70.

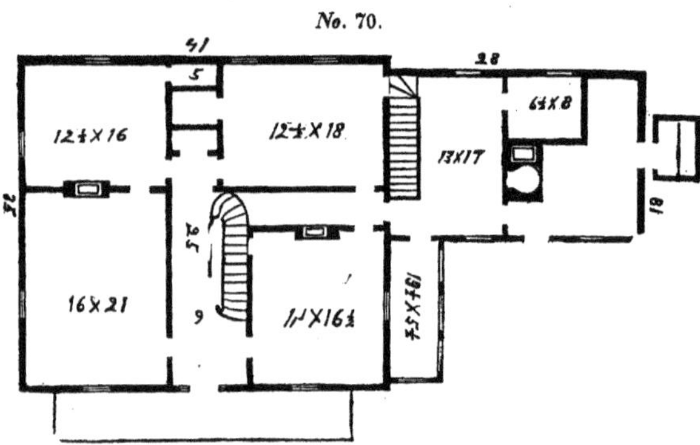

No. 70 presents the ground-plan to foregoing front and end elevations, Nos. 68 and 69.

Though the size of the main house is but thirty-five feet by forty-one feet, with an ell of twenty-eight feet by eighteen feet, for symmetry of form, size, and connection of apartments, and abundance and convenience of closet-room, this house is much approved and admired. On the ground-floor, in front, is a parlor, sixteen by twenty-one feet; hall, twenty-five by nine feet; and sitting-room, fourteen by sixteen and one half feet. In rear of parlor, library, twelve and one half by sixteen feet; and in rear of sitting-room, dining-room, twelve and one half by eighteen and one half feet, with three large closets, admirably situated for convenience; while the ell contains a kitchen, thirteen by seventeen feet, back stairway, large pantry-closet, and an ample wash and wood room. The conservatory, thirteen and one half by five and one half feet, and piazza in front, add much to the beauty and convenience of the structure, at but small increase of the expense. Estimated cost of this house, $3000.

ANTA AND ENTABLATURE.

Plate XLIV.

Here we have represented an anta and entablature suitable for this house. It is figured in minutes for the sake of convenience; and drawn to a scale of one inch to a foot.

The dark part on the left hand shows a section, or form, of all the members, &c.

No. 71.

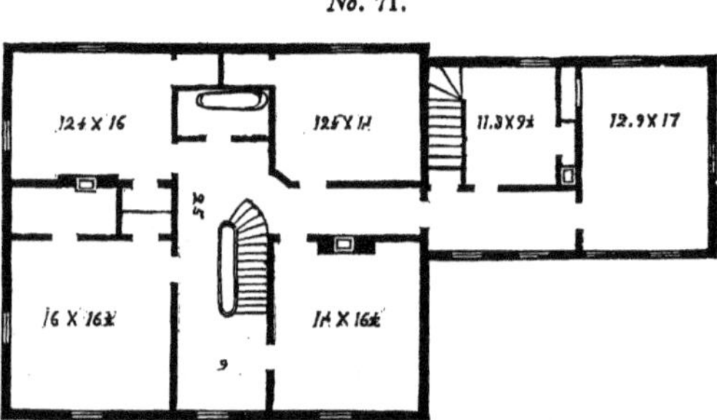

No. 71 presents the plan of the second floor, with two front chambers, sixteen and one half by sixteen feet, and fourteen by sixteen and one half feet ; two large bed-rooms, ample bath-room and closets, and in the ell a large chamber and sleeping-room, with closets from each, with width of passage-ways, and completeness of connection, which render the chambers eminently pleasant and convenient.

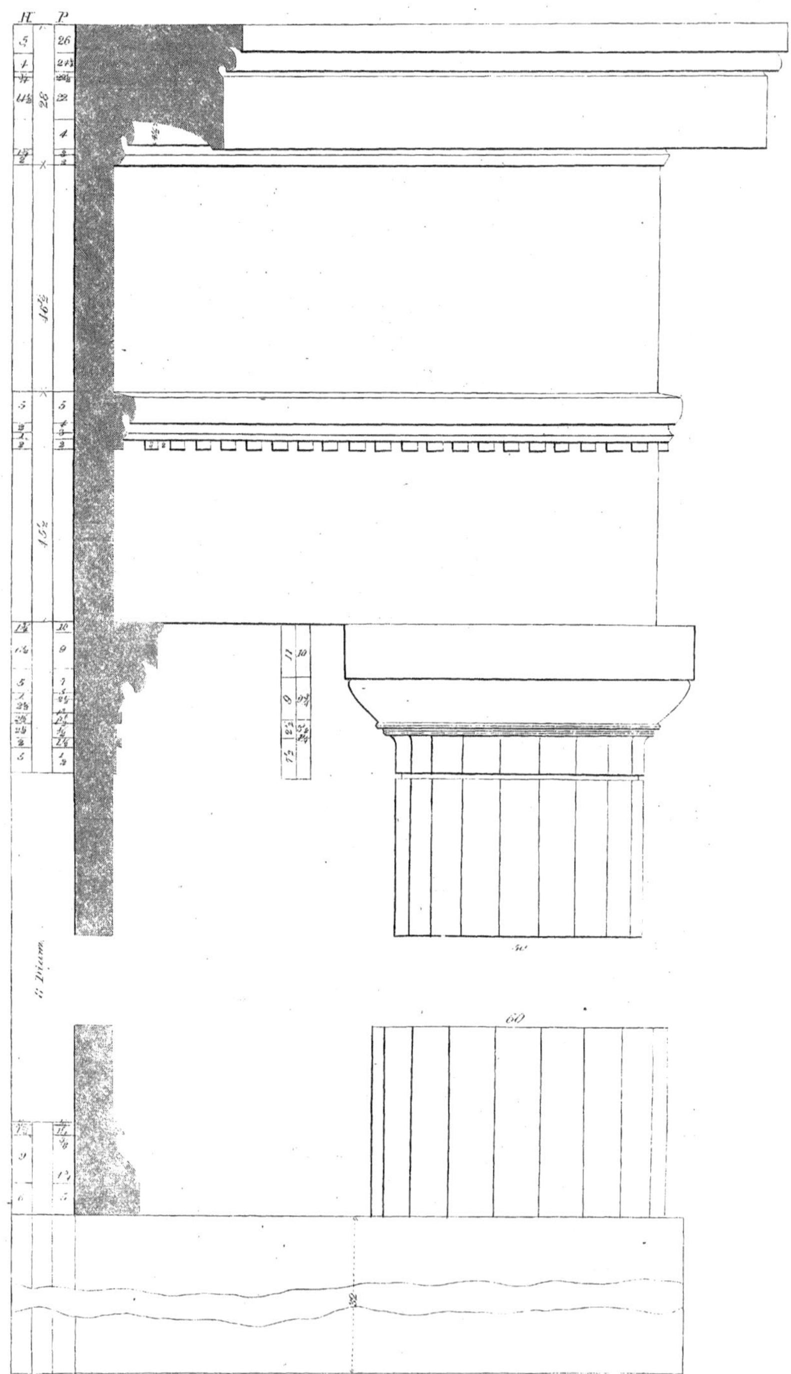

DETAILS.

PLATE XLV.

ON this plate are shown a column and entablature, designed for the portico of the Grecian house. The whole height is ten diameters; the entablature being two. The plate is figured in minutes, and drawn to a scale of one eighth of an inch to an inch. The latter division adapts it to this place; but the former is more suitable for diminishing or enlarging an order or design.

The following will show how this is done. The column at the base is sixteen inches; this is divided into 60 parts, for minutes. (See the rule given in the description of the Tuscan order.) Now, if we wish to make this larger or smaller, we should still make the same number of minutes (sixty) in the diameter of the column, and give every member the same number marked opposite under *H*, (height,) and *P*, (projection.) It follows that the members are regulated by the minutes, which are greater or less as the case may be.

This is a beautiful design for a portico, and may be executed, in almost any place, with success.

DES. III.

Wm. Brown, Archt.

DETAILS.

Plate XLVI.

Sections of an elevation of the steps, buttresses, door, door-frame, column, and of that part of the entablature which rests on the column; also, of the ceiling of the portico.

The whole is drawn to a scale of one half of an inch to a foot.

Fig. 1.

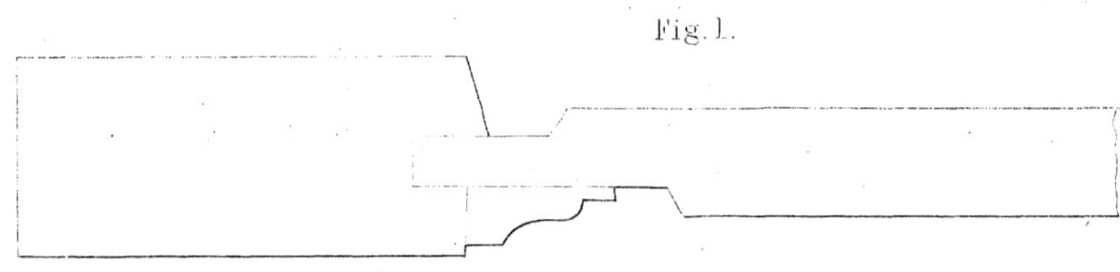

Fig. 2.

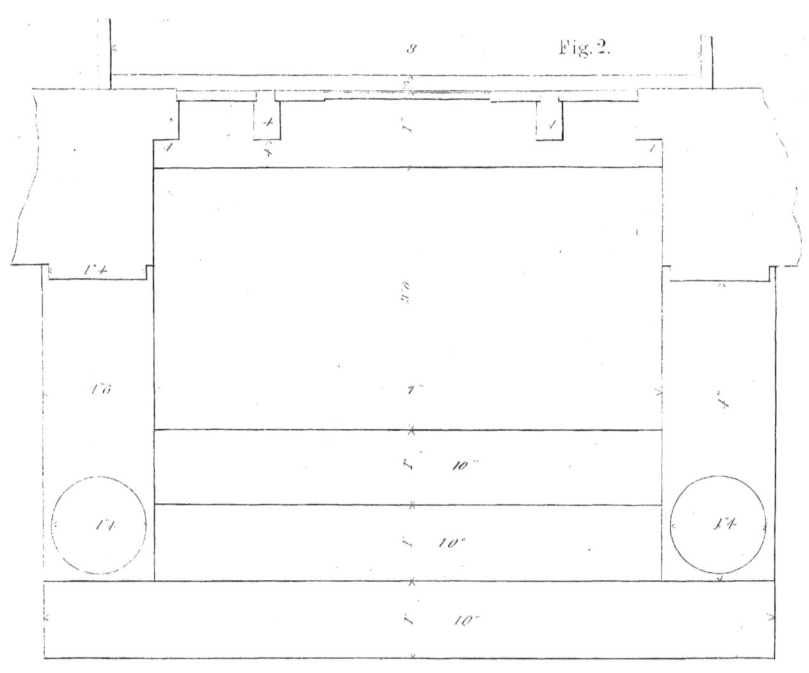

Wm. Brown, Archt. W. D. Emery, Eng.

DETAILS.

PLATE XLVII.

Fig. 1.—Sections of the door-stile, panel, and moulding, half the real size.

Fig. 2.—A plan of the portico, shown in the preceding plate, drawn to the same scale.

Fig. 1.

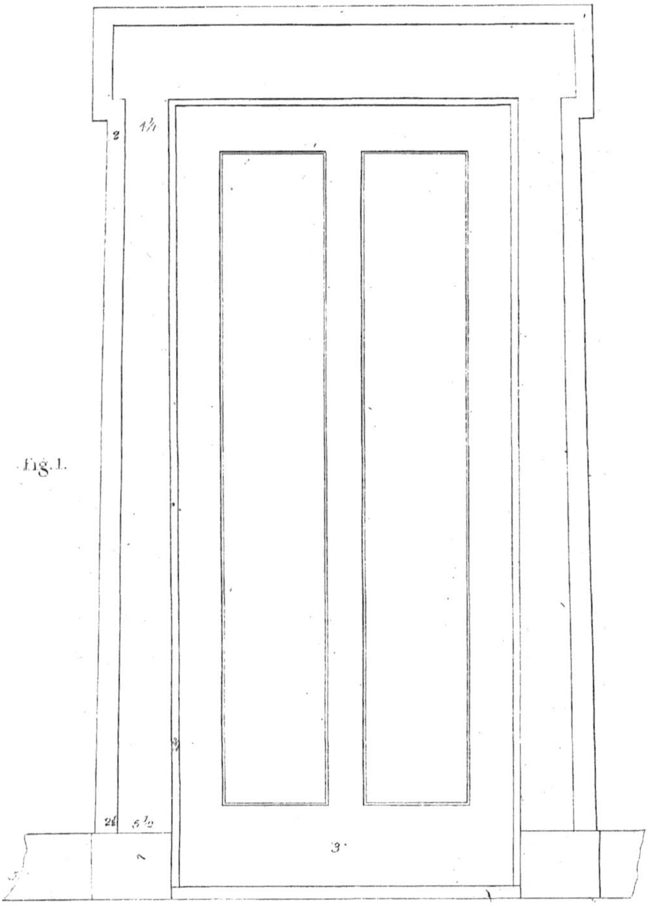

Fig. 2.

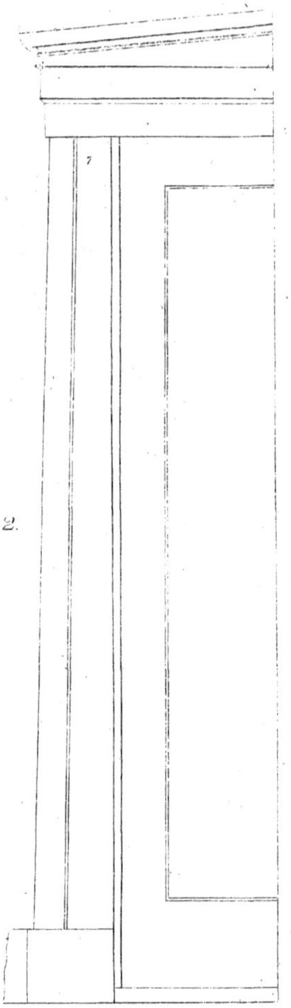

Fig. 3.

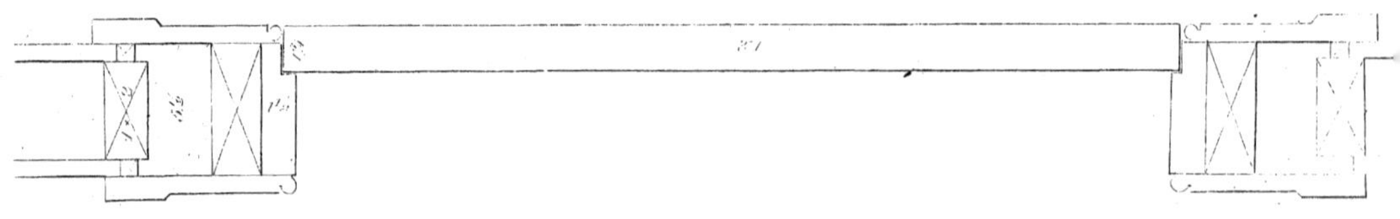

Wm. Brown, Archt.

W. B. Emery, Eng.

DETAILS.

Plate XLVIII.

Figs. 1 and 2 are designs for inside doors and their finish, which are suitable for this house, drawn to a scale of three fourths of an inch to a foot.

Fig. 3.—A plan of a door-frame with the door closed, drawn to a scale of one and a half inches to a foot.

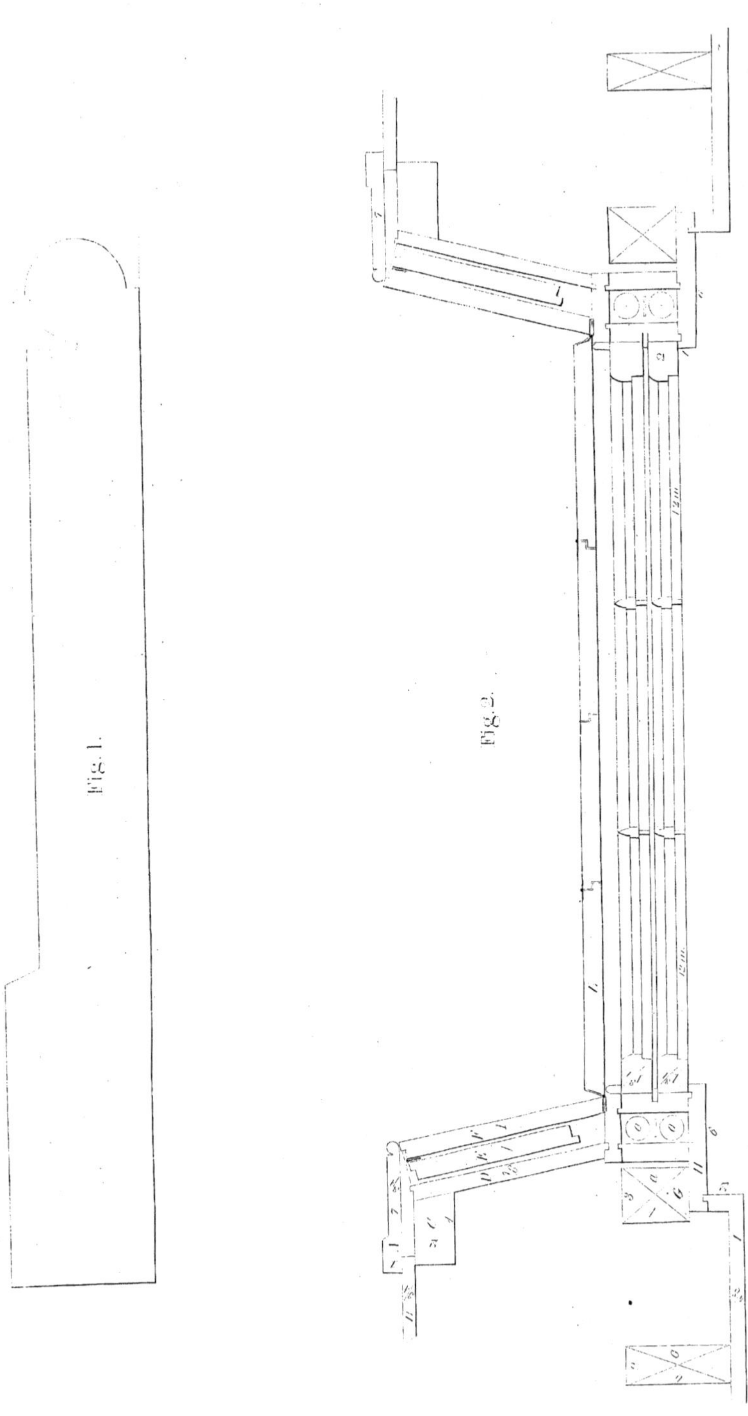
Fig. 1.
Fig. 2.
12 in.
12 in.

DETAILS.

PLATE XLIX.

Fig. 1.—An architrave of full size for the preceding plate, which we have executed in several instances; and it has never failed, in any suitable position, to give a good effect.

Fig. 2.—Section of a window, with shutters and all the appendages in detail, drawn to a scale of one inch and a half to a foot. *A*, architrave; *B*, plastering; *C*, stud; *D*, back-lining; *E*, back-flap; *F*, box-leaf of shutters; *GG*, studs; *OO*, weights; *H*, face-lining; *I*, sheathing; *L*, shutters closed.

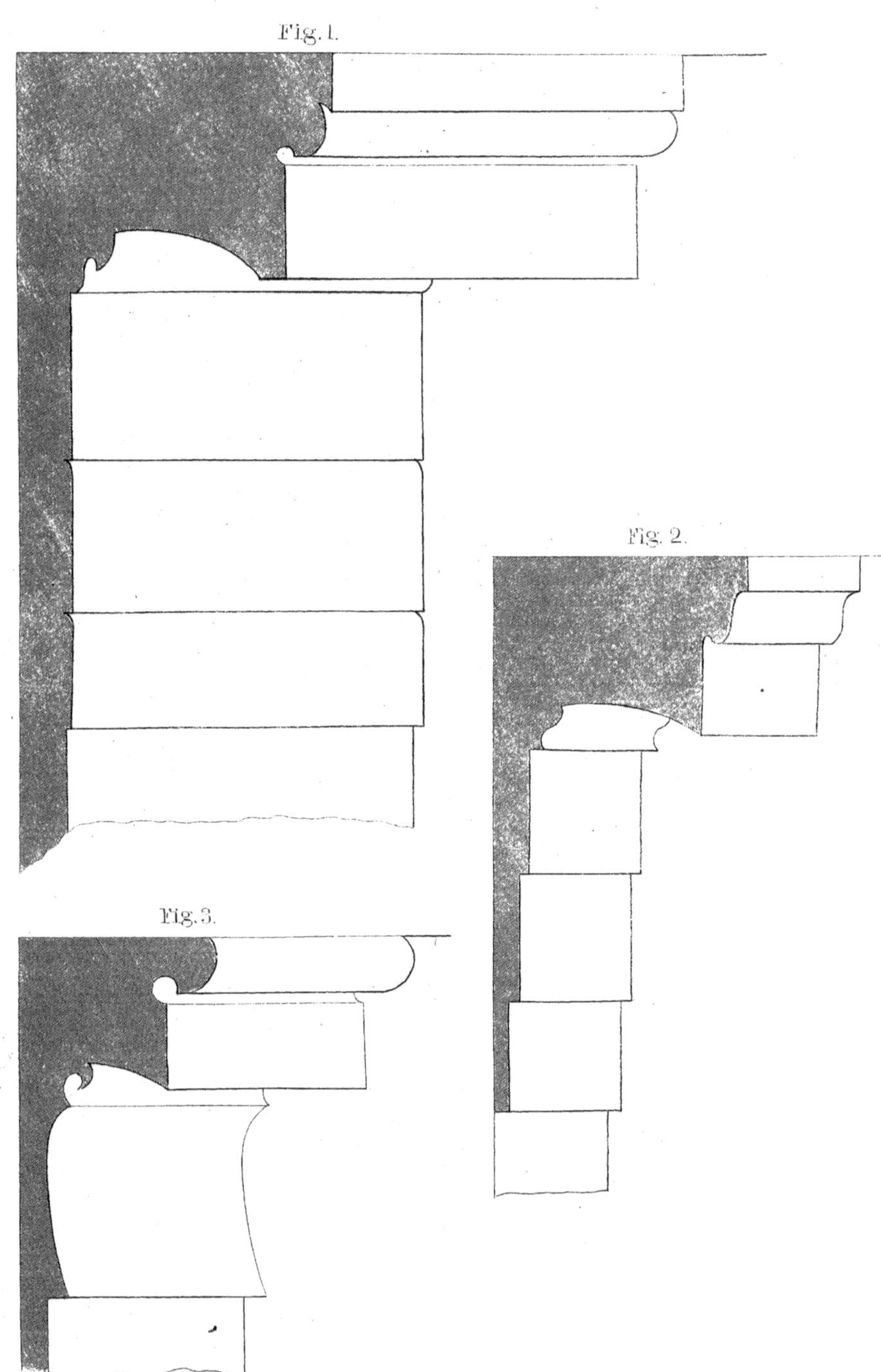

Wm. Brown, Archt.

STUCCO CORNICES.

Plate L.

On this plate are three designs for stucco cornices.

Fig. 1.—Cornice for the drawing-room.

Fig. 2.—Cornice for the parlor.

Fig. 3.—Cornice for the vestibule and hall.

These designs are drawn to a scale of three inches to a foot.

Fig. 1.

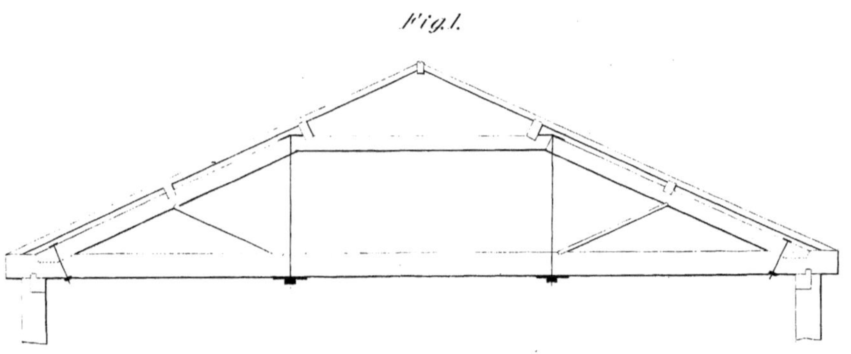

Fig. 2.

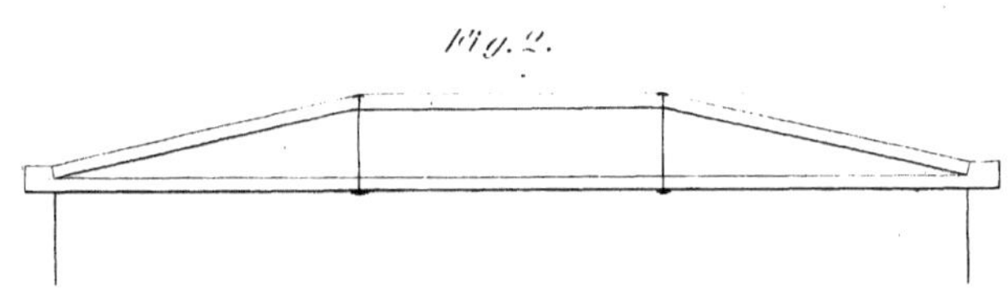

Fig. 3.

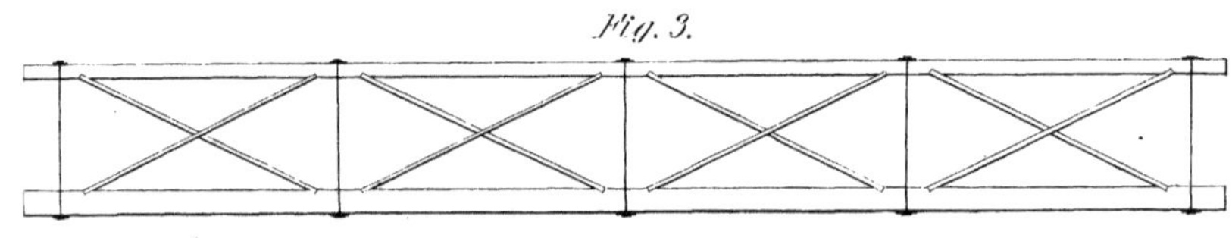

Fig. 1.

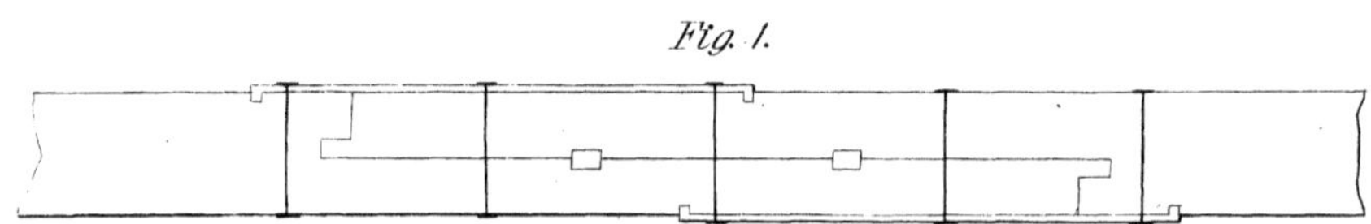

Wm. Brown Archt.

CARPENTRY.

Plate LI.

Fig. 1 is an example of a truss roof of forty feet span. The queen-posts are represented to be made of iron, instead of wood, as is usually the case. The particular advantage of the former mode over the latter is this: the settling of the timbers caused by the shrinking of the posts is done away with. The sizes of all the timbers, &c., suitable for this roof, are given below. This kind of truss may be extended to forty-five feet with safety.

Sizes of materials to be used in this truss:

Tie-beam, ...	12 × 10
Principal rafter, ...	9 × 8
Straining beams, ...	9 × 8
Struts, ...	8 × 2
Purlins, ...	8 × 6
Jack rafters, ...	6 × 2
Iron queen-posts, ...	1¼ round.
Bolts at the foot of the rafters, ...	⅞ "
Coving joists, ...	8 × 3

We will here observe, that "the weight of the timber and boarding of the roof is equal to about five pounds on each superficial foot, and the weight of the slates, eleven pounds; these sums, added together, make sixteen pounds, which is the permanent load on each superficial foot."

Fig. 2 is designed for a truss of thirty feet span. It may be employed in any place where no very great strength is required. Timber which is six inches by ten will be about the right size for this truss. The mode of construction will be readily understood by inspection of the figure.

Fig. 3 represents a gallery truss of forty feet span, which will need no explanation. The sizes of the timbers to be used in *this* kind of truss may be as follows:

Lower timbers, ...	10 × 8
Struts, ...	8 × 2
Upper timbers, ...	8 × 8
Iron rods, ...	1 round.

Fig. 4 is designed for scarfing beams where great nicety is required. It will be observed that iron plates are represented on two sides.

The first three figures on this plate are drawn to a scale of one eighth of an inch to a foot.

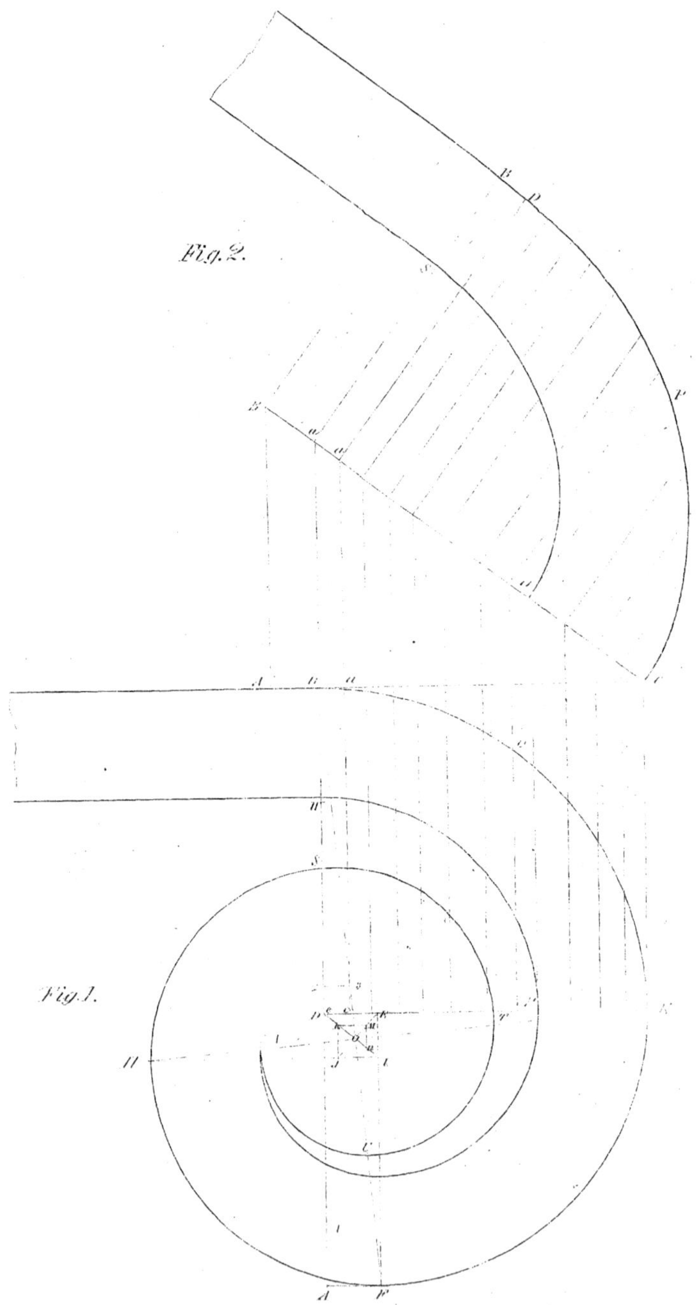
Fig.2.
Fig.1.

Plate LII.

Fig. 1 shows a method of drawing a scroll for stairs.

Let *AB* be the given breadth, which is here sixteen inches; divide *AB* into eleven equal parts, make *AF* equal to one of those parts, and join *BF;* then bisect *BA*, and *BF*, at 2 3, in the centre of *BA;* make 2 *D* equal to 2 3; then, with the dividers on *D*, with a radius of *DB*, intersect *DK;* draw *DK* perpendicular to *AB*, and *HK* at right angles to *BF*, intersecting *BF* at *o;* draw *EF* parallel to *AB;* draw the diagonals *DI EJ*, which will form the centres; then, with one foot of the dividers on *D*, describe the arc *BK;* and on *E* the arc *KF;* and on *I* the arc *FH;* and on *J* the arc *HS;* and on *L* the arc *ST;* and on *M* forming the arc *TU;* and on *R* the arc *UV;* which will complete the spiral curve. Proceed with the same centres to obtain the inside of the rail, commencing at *W*.

Fig. 2 shows the method of obtaining the face mould for a scroll.

Let *ABC* be the pitch board; make *aB* in Fig. 2 equal to *BD* in Fig. 1, also *aD* in Fig. 2 equal to *ae* in Fig. 1. Proceed with all the ordinates in the same manner, both on the inner and outer edges of the rail; then trace the curve line *BC*, and *SO*, and we have the mould complete.

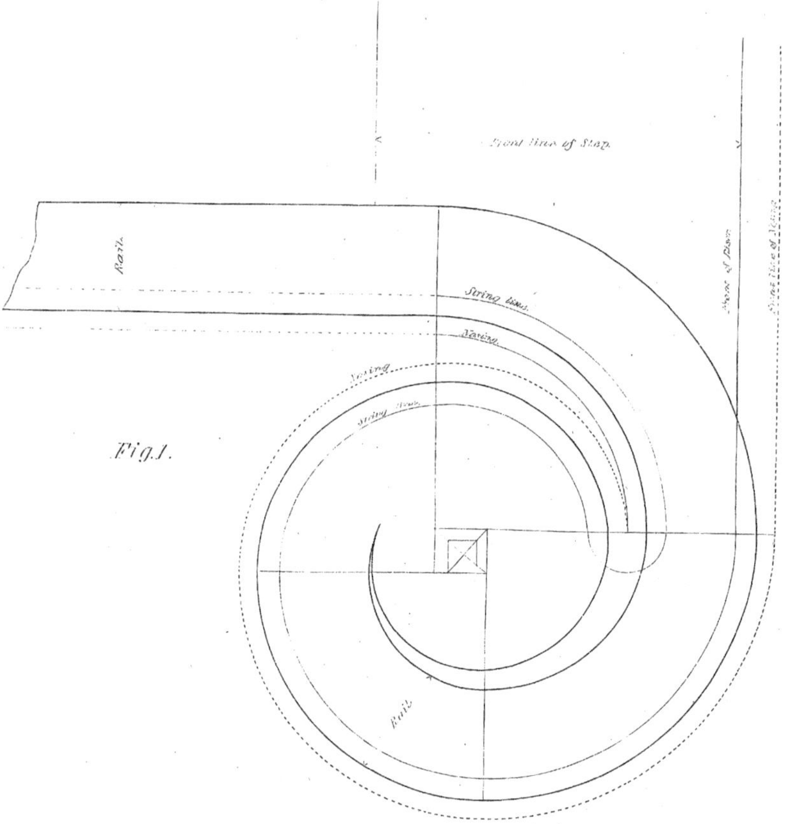

Front line of Step.

Rail.

String lines.

Nosing.

Front of Riser.

Front line of Nosing.

Fig. 1.

Fig. 2.

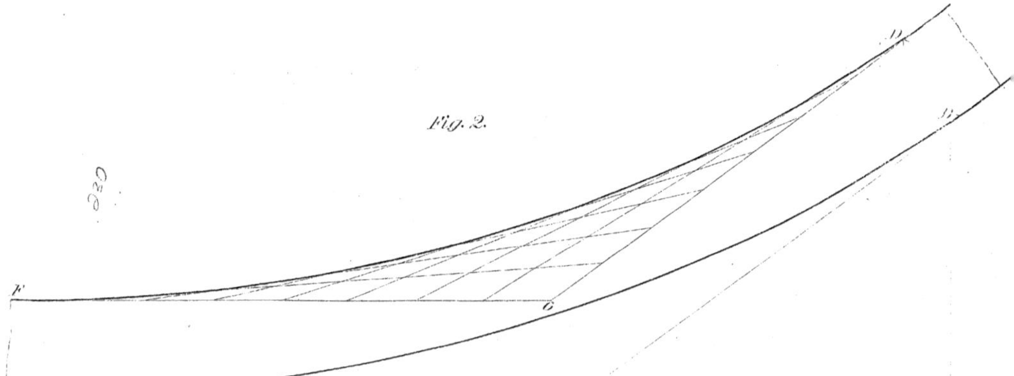

D

B

F

G

E

A

C

230

Plate LIII.

Fig. 1 shows the method of forming a curtail step. It is drawn on the same scale of the scroll, which is one quarter the full size; the centres are the same as in the scroll. We think this will be readily understood without further explanation, as the lines are described on the plate.

Fig. 2 shows the method of obtaining the falling mould of the scroll in the preceding plate. Let *ABC* be the *pitch board,* and *EC* the *stretchout* from *B* to *F*, Fig. 1 of the preceding plate. Then set up from *B* to *D*, and *E* to *F*, the depth of the rail. Draw *DG* parallel to *BA*, and *FG* parallel to *EA*; divide *FG* and *DG* each into an equal number of parts; then draw intersecting lines as shown in the drawings, and trace the curve line *FD*, and we have the upper edge of the mould; the lower edge may be obtained by gauging.

PLATE LIV.

ON plate 54, *A B*, Fig. 1 being the ground-plan of the semi-circular part, having a portion of straight rail attached.

At *a b* and *c d* describe the points *e* and *f*, and from the point *e f* draw lines through *a b* and *c d* to the tangent lines *n m* and *j k*, which lines will be the stretch-outs of the concave and convex semi-circumference of the given plan. To obtain the concave falling-mould, Fig. 2, draw the horizontal line *m b* equal to the concave stretch-out: at the point *b* place the pitch-board *b n r*. Let *m a* be equal to the height of the riser, and divide it into four equal parts: the first and third part gives the point *x* and *e;* at the point *a b* place the pitch-board *a j l;* then draw the lines *j e*, *e x*, and *x v;* then set up the thickness of the rail, and then apply the length of the straight part *s a* and *y b*, of the ground-plan, Fig. 1, to the base of the pitch-boards from *n* to *h*, and *a* to *f;* then erect the perpendiculars, and square across the rail, as is represented, and you have the mould complete. To obtain the joint in the centre of the semi-circular part, let drop the line *G H*, passing through the centres of the concave and convex falling mould, square across the mould, and the line will be the required joint; draw the lines *u u*, and *z z*, which will be the required overwood; apply the overwood to the ground-plan, Fig. 1; then draw the lines *C O*, touching *v* and *z d*, and *O Z*, and *d s* will be the height for the parts *B* and *A* of said mould. The easings are formed as represented by the intersecting lines.

The convex falling-mould, Fig. 3, is obtained in the same manner as the concave at Fig. 2.

Let *j d*, the base Fig. 3, be equal to *j k*, the stretch-out in Fig. 1; *j c* is equal to the height of a rise of *d w*, and *c r* equal to the straight part, as in Fig. 2; the easings and the overwood are obtained in the same manner as before, and you will have your convex falling-mould.

How to obtain the face-moulds, Fig. 4 and 5, from the ground-plan.

At the part *B*, Fig. 1, draw the chord-line 5 9 touching the points *y z*, including the over-wood. Erect perpendicular lines from said chord-lines at 5 *y* 6 7 8 *Z* and 9, through the points *w y d b* and *Z;* draw *O Y* parallel to the chord-line; then take the height, *O Z*, Fig. 2, and apply it from *O* to *Z*, Fig. 4; then draw 5 9, touching the point *y* at the angles; *z y* is the pitch-bevel obtained. Draw lines at right angles to 9 5, and from the points 5 6 7 8 9; then take the several distances, 5 *W*, 6 *d*, 7 *b*, 8 4 4, and 9 *X*, from the chord-

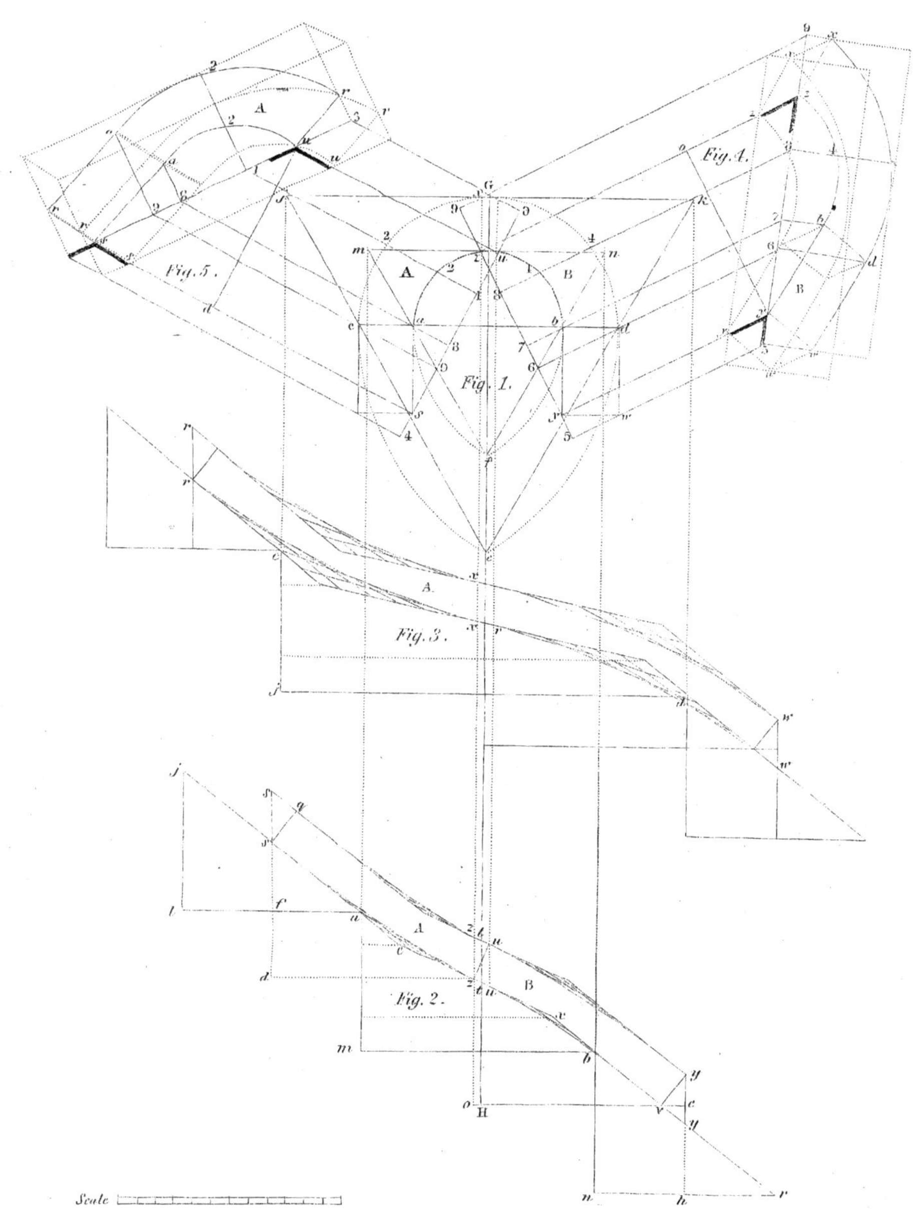

Fig. 5.
Fig. 4.
Fig. 1.
Fig. 3.
Fig. 2.
Scale

Pl.

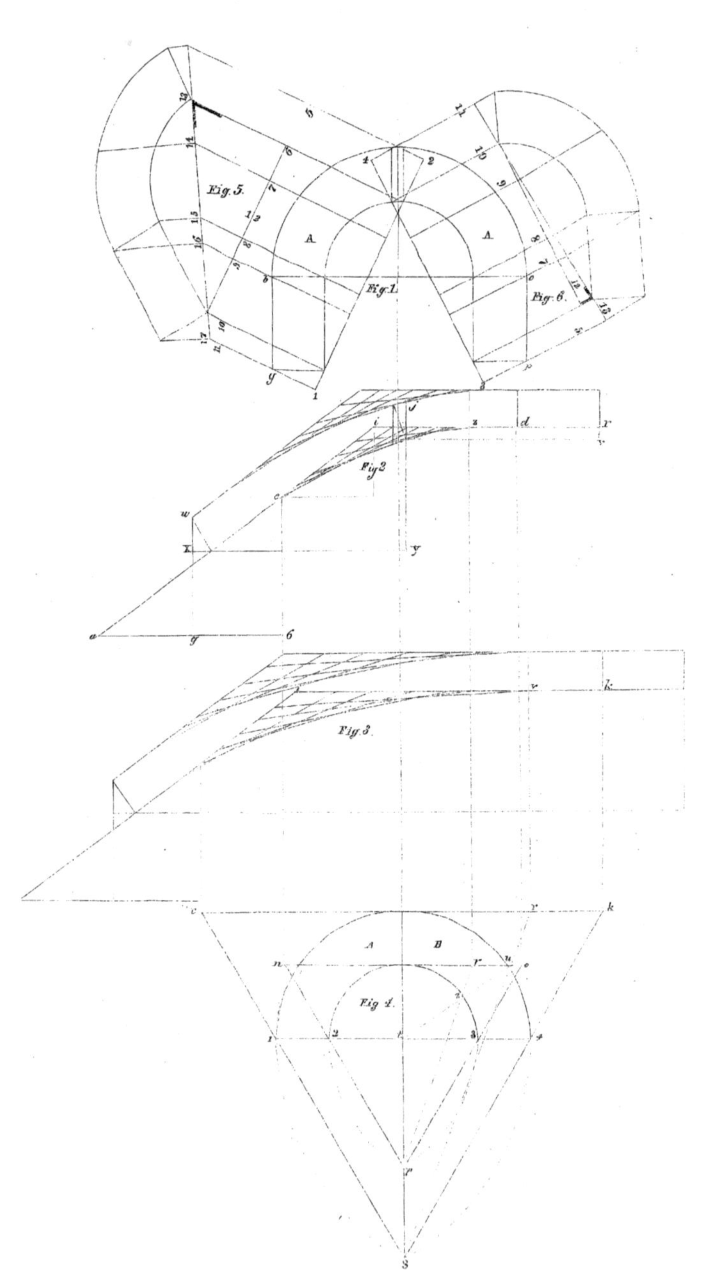

line, Fig. 1, and apply them upon the lines carried out at right angles from 5 9 from the points 5 6 7 8 and 9, to *w d b* 44 and *x*; draw the line *x Z*, which will be the end of the required mould.

The points *z* 4 *b* and *x* 4 *d* being obtained, describe the arcs through them, and *b y* and *d w* will be the length at the straight part, and *y w* the end of the required mould.

The face-mould, Fig. 5, is obtained in the same manner as in Fig. 4, the straight part being thrown up, and the height from the parallel lines at *d* to the hypothenuse at *s* being obtained at *d s*, Fig. 2.

The diagrams 4 and 5 show the manner of applying the face-moulds to both sides of the plank.

From the part *z* and *y*, Fig. 4, and *u* and *S*, Fig. 5, at the inner edge of the plank, the pitch-bevels being obtained and applied across the edge *z y*, Fig. 4, and *u s*, Fig. 5, will be the angle of inclination to the rail-pieces. Then tracing the line of the mould on both sides of the plank; then cut out your rail-piece; then it will be ready for the application of the falling-moulds.

Take the part *B*, Fig. 2, of the concave falling-mould, which is of paper, and apply it to the concave edge of the rail-piece at Fig. 4, having the plumb-lines *z z* of the over-wood, Fig. 2, applied to the lines of the pitch-bevels *z z* and *y y*, then the plumb-line *y y* of said mould will coincide with the line *y y* of the pitch-bevel; then mark the joints *y v* and *u z*, and on the upper edge at *y*, and the lower edge at *z*, of said joints, square across the ends of said rail-piece.

Then apply the convex mould to the convex side, and you will have the required piece.

The upper wreath at *A*, Fig. 5, is formed in the same manner as *B*, Fig. 4.

Plate LV.

Shows the manner of drawing a continued rail to a straight flight of stairs, easing up on the landing.

Let *A A*, Fig. 1, be the ground-plan of the circular part of the rail, with a portion of the straight rail attached, so as to bring the joint on the straight part of rail.

A B, Fig. 4, shows the manner of obtaining the stretch-out of the semi-circular part: *a b c d* is the diameters of the concave and convex semi-circumference of the rail.

1, 2, 3, and 4, as centres; draw the arcs intersecting at *P* and *S;* then draw the tangent lines *n o e k* of the concave and convex sides of the given plan. From the point *P* draw lines through 2 and 3, until it intersect at *n* and *o;* also from *S* through 1 and 4, until it intersects at *e* and *k;* then *N O* and *e k* will be the stretch-outs of the two semi-circular lines.

It will be observed that *A B*, Fig. 4, is the same as *A A*, Fig 1. Fig. 4 is to show the manner of obtaining the different points and their stretch-outs.

To obtain the falling-mould for the concave stretch-outs, Fig. 2 *N* and *O*, Fig. 4, erect perpendicular from the point *n* and *O* of the concave stretch-out to *c* and *d;* at the points *c*, place the upper angle of the pitch-board *a b c* and *c e*, the line of floor; draw *e i* equal to half a rise at right angle to *C e;* then draw the hypothenuse, *a I* and *I r*, parallel to the top of floor.

Let *d r* be equal to the straight part *O P*, of Fig. 1.

We will now form the easing. From the angle at *i*, up on the hypothenuse, measure off eight inches in length, which divide into six equal parts. Then take four of these parts, and apply it upon the opposite side of the angle at *I*, and then divide said distance into six equal parts; then draw intersecting lines, and the easing will be formed for the under side of the rail. Then set up the depth of the rail, square across it at each extremity of said easings, and from the points upon the upper side of the rail the upper easing may be formed.

Take the length of the straight part *g b* of Fig. 1, and apply it upon the base of the pitch-board *b* to *g*, Fig. 2.

Erect the perpendicular *g w*, and form *w* square across the rail, which line will be the joint; the joint at *J* in the centre is obtained by squaring across the rail at *j T;* then draw lines parallel to the perpendicular at *j* and *T*, which lines will be the over-wood necessary for the joints; which over-wood must be applied to the joint in Fig. 1, as readily perceived, at *r* square across the rail, which is the terminating joint.

From the lower joint draw *x y j v*, which is the given height for each piece.

The convex falling-mould, Fig. 3, is obtained in the same manner, from *e k*, the convex stretch-out, Fig. 4, as Fig. 2 was obtained.

To form the easing upon convex falling-mould, Fig. 3, so that it may coincide with the concave easing Fig. 2, take the distance from *z*, at the termination of the easing, to *d* at Fig. 2, and apply it up on the concave stretch-out from *O* to *r*, Fig. 4; then draw the line *r P*, and through its intersection with the concave at *z*, on the semi-circumference, draw *T U*, from the centre *T* to the convex semi-circumference *U;* then draw *s v* through the point of intersection at *u*, and *v k* will be the required distance. Apply said distance

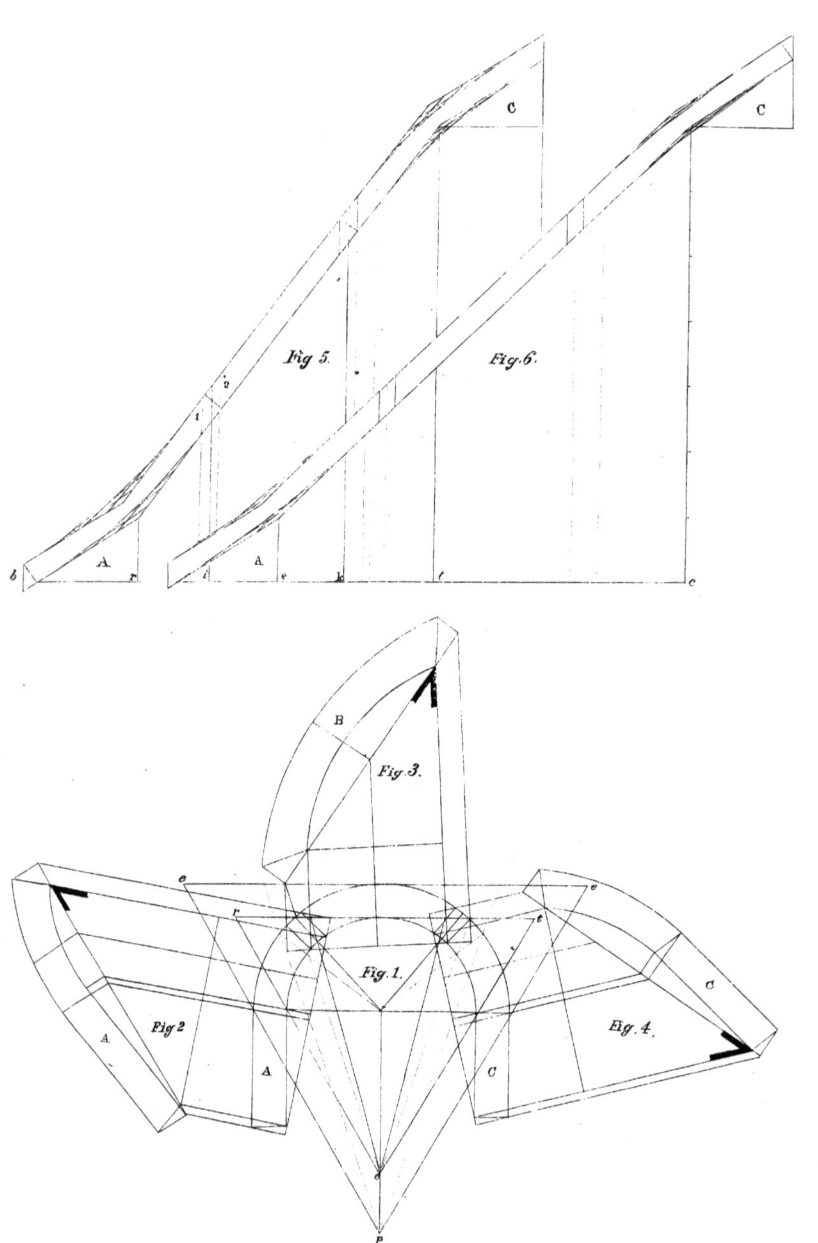
Fig 5.
Fig. 6.
C
C
A
A
b
r
i
e
k
t
c
1
2
Fig. 3.
B
Fig. 1.
Fig 2
A
A
Fig. 4.
C
C
e
r
e
t
o
P

DETAILS.

Plate XLVII.

Fig. 1.—Sections of the door-stile, panel, and moulding, half the real size.

Fig. 2.—A plan of the portico, shown in the preceding plate, drawn to the same scale.

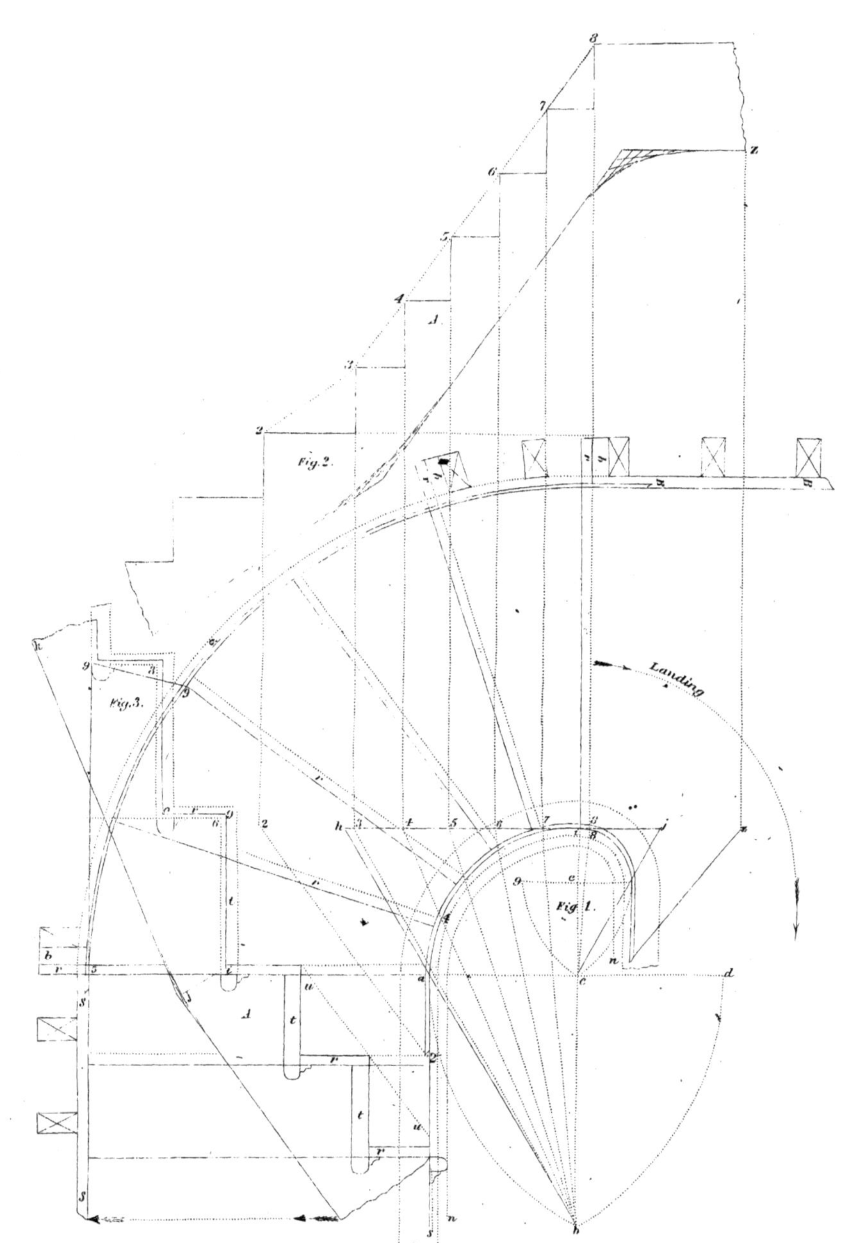

Fig. 2.
Fig. 3.
Fig 1.
Landing

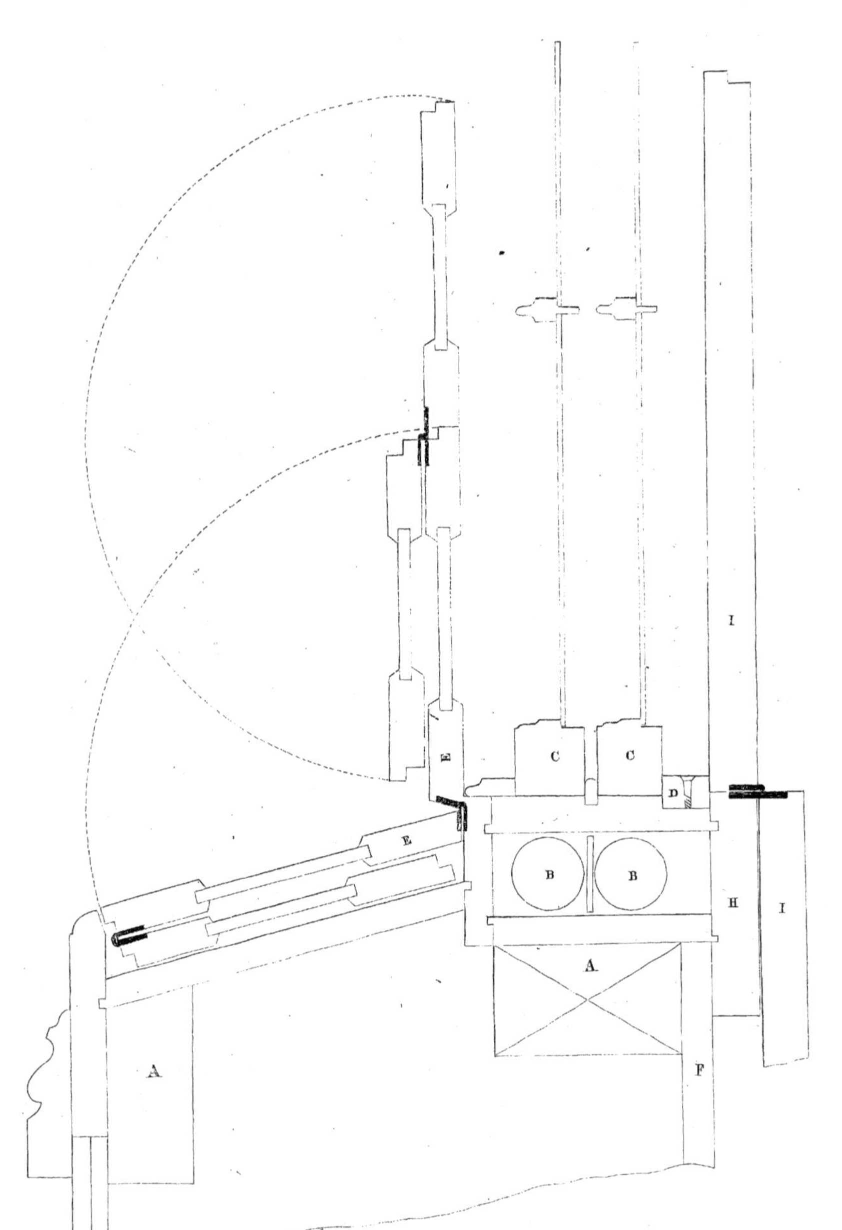

E
C
C
D
E
B
B
H
I
I
A
A
F

DETAILS.

PLATE XLVIII.

Figs. 1 and 2 are designs for inside doors and their finish, which are suitable for this house, drawn to a scale of three fourths of an inch to a foot.

Fig. 3.—A plan of a door-frame with the door closed, drawn to a scale of one and a half inches to a foot.

PLT. LIX

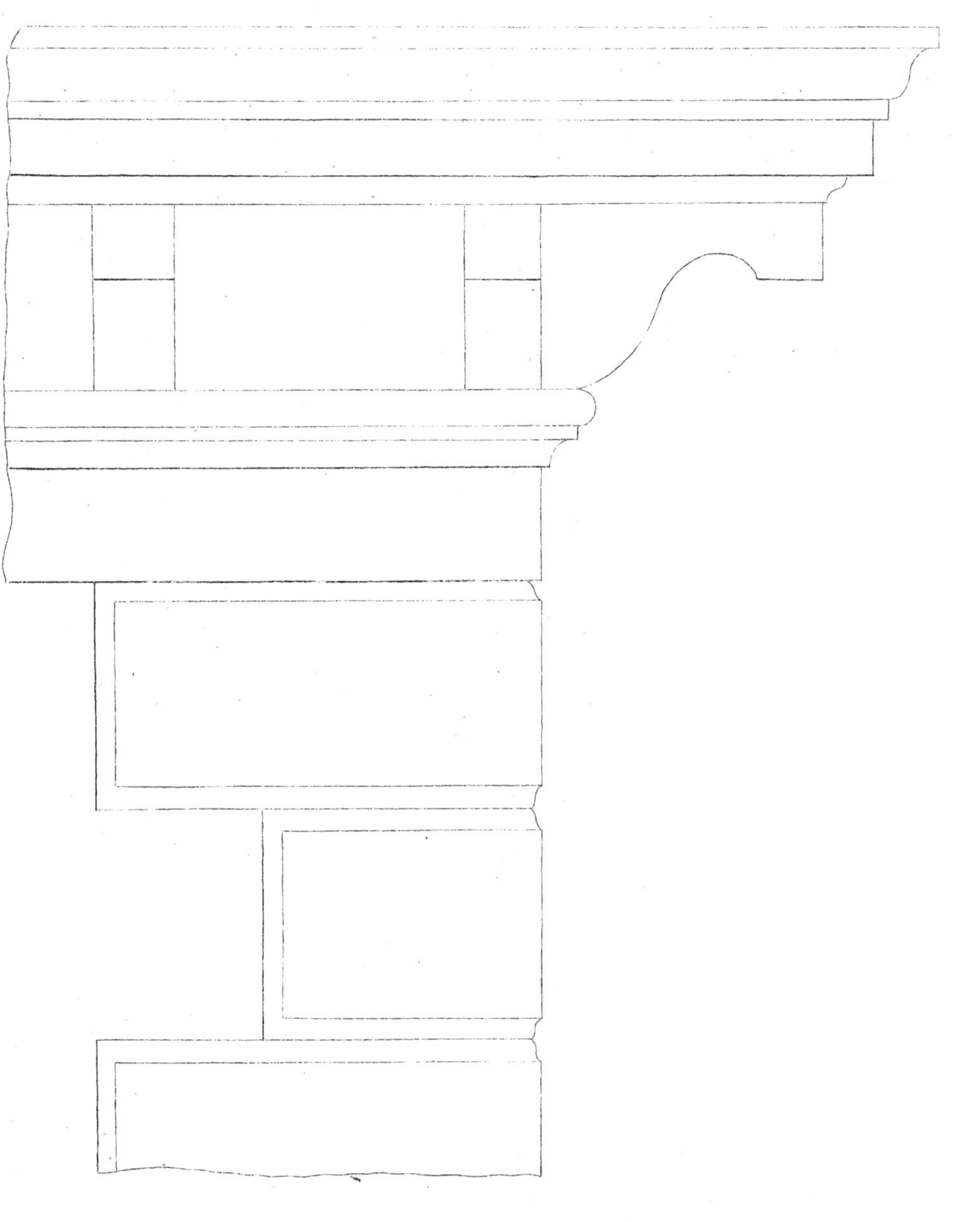

12 in 1 2 Ft.

12 in. 1 2 Ft.

PLT. LX

12 in 1 2 Ft.

1
2
3

PLT. LXIV

1 2 3

1
2
3

PLT. LXV

3 Ft 2 1 12 in

12 in
1
2
3 Ft.

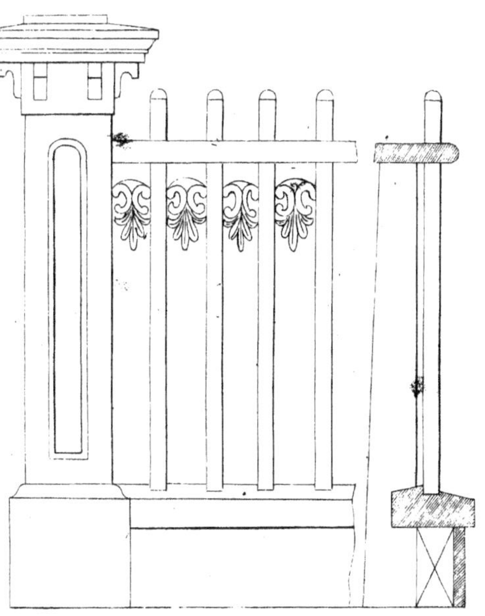

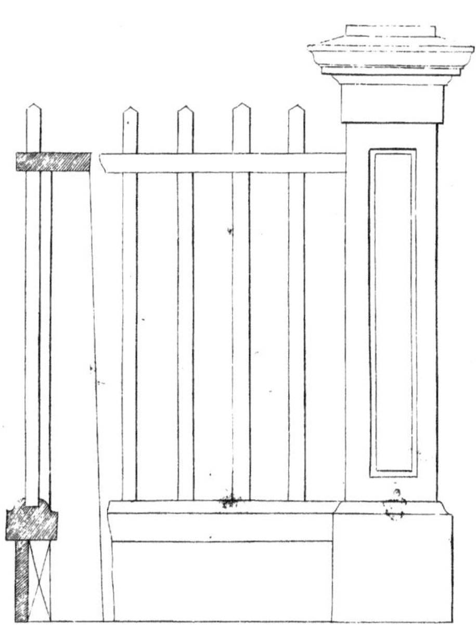

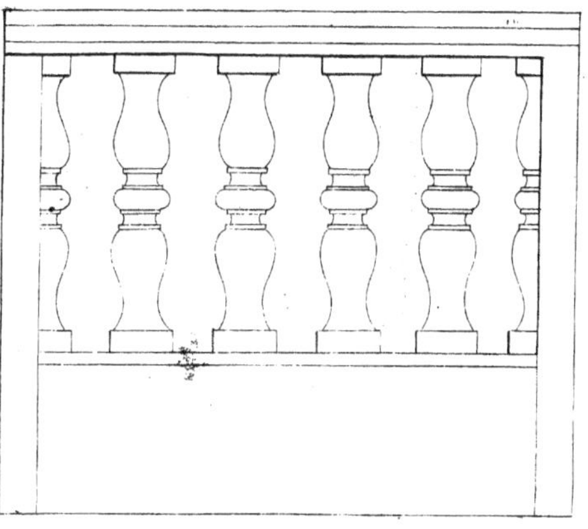

Diam.	Circum.	Area.	Side of equal Square.	Diam.	Circum.	Area.	Side of equal Square.
22 in.	69·115	380·133	19·496	36 in.	113·097	1017·87	31·903
¼	69·900	388·822	19·718	¼	113·883	1032·06	32·124
½	70·686	397·608	19·939	½	114·668	1046·39	32·346
23 in.	72·256	415·476	20·382	37 in.	116·239	1075·21	32·789
¼	73·042	424·557	20·604	¼	117·024	1089·79	33·011
½	73·827	433·731	20·825	½	117·810	1104·46	33·232
24 in.	75·398	452·390	21·268	38 in.	119·380	1134·11	33·675
¼	76·183	461·864	21·490	¼	120·166	1149·08	33·897
½	76·969	471·436	21·712	½	120·951	1164·15	34·118
25 in.	78·540	490·875	22·155	39 in.	122·522	1194·59	34·561
¼	79·325	500·741	22·376	¼	123·307	1209·95	34·783
½	80·110	510·706	22·598	½	124·093	1225·42	35·005
26 in.	81·681	530·930	23·041	40 in.	125·664	1256·64	35·448
¼	82·467	541·189	23·062	¼	126·449	1272·39	35·669
½	83·252	551·547	23·484	½	127·234	1288·25	35·891
27 in.	84·823	572·556	23·927	41 in.	128·805	1320·25	36·334
¼	85·608	583·208	24·149	¼	129·591	1336·40	36·555
½	86·394	593·958	24·370	½	130·376	1352·65	36·777
28 in.	87·964	615·753	24·813	42 in.	131·947	1385·44	37·220
¼	88·750	626·798	25·035	¼	132·732	1401·98	37·442
½	89·535	637·941	25·256	½	133·518	1418·62	37·663
29 in.	91·106	660·521	25·699	43 in.	135·088	1452·20	38·106
¼	91·891	671·958	25·921	¼	135·874	1469·13	38·328
½	92·677	683·494	26·143	½	136·659	1486·17	38·549
30 in.	94·248	706·860	26·586	44 in.	138·230	1520·53	38·993
¼	95·033	718·690	26·807	¼	139·015	1537·86	39·214
½	95·818	730·618	27·029	½	139·801	1555·28	39·436
31 in.	97·389	754·769	27·472	45 in.	141·372	1590·43	39·879
¼	98·175	766·992	27·693	¼	142·157	1608·15	40·110
½	98·968	779·313	27·915	½	142·942	1625·97	40·322
32 in.	100·531	804·249	28·358	46 in.	144·513	1661·90	40·765
¼	101·316	816·865	28·580	¼	145·299	1680·01	40·986
½	102·102	829·578	28·801	½	146·084	1698·23	41·208
33 in.	103·672	855·30	29·244	47 in.	147·655	1754·94	41·651
¼	104·458	868·30	29·466	¼	148·440	1753·45	41·873
½	105·243	881·41	29·687	½	149·226	1772·05	42·094
34 in.	106·814	907·92	30·131	48 in.	150·796	1809·56	42·537
¼	107·599	921·32	30·352	¼	151·582	1828·46	42·759
½	108·385	934·82	30·574	½	152·367	1847·45	42·980
35 in.	109·956	962·11	31·017	49 in.	153·938	1885·74	43·423
¼	110·741	975·90	31·238	¼	154·723	1905·03	43·645
½	111·526	989·80	31·460	½	155·509	1924·42	43·867

MISCELLANEOUS.

THE following are the results of experiments made by Mr. Emerson, which state the load that may be safely borne by a square inch rod of each:

	Pounds Avoirdupois.
Iron rod, an inch square, will bear,	76,400
Brass,	35,600
Hempen rope,	19,600
Ivory,	15,700
Oak, box, yew, plum-tree,	7,850
Elm, ash, beech,	6,070
Walnut, plum,	5,360
Red pine, holly, elder, plum, crab,	5,000
Cherry, hazel,	4,760
Alder, asp, birch, willow,	4,290
Lead,	430
Free-stone,	914

ACTUAL COHESION.

Gold Cast,	24,000 / 20,000
Silver Cast,	40,000 / 43,000
Copper Cast,	28,700
Steel Bar, Soft,	120,000
Steel Bar, Razor tempered,	150,000
Lead Cast,	860
Zinc,	2,600

CIRCLES AND DIAMETERS.

To find the circumference of a circle, the diameter being given; or, to find the diameter, the circumference being given, we have the following

RULE.

Multiply 3.1416 by the diameter, and the product will be the circumference; or,

Divide the circumference by 3.1416, and the quotient is the diameter.

Note.—As 22 is to 7, so is the circumference to the diameter; or, as 7 is to 22, so is the diameter to the circumference.

EXAMPLES.

1. What is the circumference of a circle whose diameter is 15?

$$3.1416 \times 15 = 47.124 = \textit{circumference.}$$

2. What is the diameter of a circle whose circumference is 179?

$$\frac{179.000}{3.1416} = 56.97 = \textit{diameter.}$$

3. Required the circumference of a circle whose diameter is 30 feet.
Ans. 94.248.

4. Find the circumference of a circle whose diameter is 13 feet.
Ans. 40.84.

5. Required the diameter of a circle whose circumference is 24884.6136.
Ans. 7921.

6. The circumference of a circle being 37.6992, what is the diameter?
Ans. 12.

The following Table, taken from the "Mechanic's Own Book," contains diameters and circumferences in inches and parts, from half an inch to 65 inches.

Diameter in inches & half.	Circumference in inches and parts.	Diameter in inches & half.	Circumference in inches and parts.	Diameter in inches & half.	Circumference in inches and parts.	Diameter in inches & half.	Circumference in inches and parts.	Diameter in inches & half.	Circumference in inches and parts.
½	1.57	7½	23.56	14½	45.55	21½	67.54	28½	89.53
1	3.14	8	25.13	15	47.12	22	69.11	29	91.1
1½	4.71	8½	26.7	15½	48.70	22½	70.7	29½	92.67
2	6.28	9	28.27	16	50.26	23	72.25	30	94.28
2½	7.85	9½	29.84	16½	51.83	23½	73.82	30½	95.81
3	9.42	10	31.4	17	53.40	24	75.4	31	97.39
3½	10.99	10½	32.98	17½	54.97	24½	76.9	31½	98.96
4	12.56	11	34.55	18	56.54	25	78.54	32	100.53
4½	14.13	11½	36.12	18½	58.11	25½	80.11	32½	102.1
5	15.7	12	37.70	19	59.69	26	81.68	33	103.67
5½	17.28	12½	39.27	19½	61.26	26½	83.25	33½	105.24
6	18.85	13	40.84	20	62.8	27	84.82	34	106.81
6½	20.42	13½	42.4	20½	64.4	27½	86.39	34½	108.38
7	21.99	14	43.98	21	65.97	28	87.96	35	109.95

Diameter in inches & half.	Circumference in inches and parts.	Diameter in inches & half.	Circumference in inches and parts.	Diameter in inches & half.	Circumference in inches and parts.	Diameter in inches & half.	Circumference in inches and parts.	Diameter in inches & half.	Circumference in inches and parts.
35½	111.52	41½	130.37	47½	149.22	53½	168.	59½	186.92
36	113.00	42	131.94	48	150.79	54	169.64	60	188.49
36½	114.66	42½	133.51	48½	152.36	54½	171.21	60½	190.
37	116.23	43	135.	49	153.93	55	172.78	61	191.63
37½	117.81	43½	136.65	49½	155.5	55½	174.35	61½	193.2
38	119.38	44	138.23	50	157.	56	175.92	62	194.77
38½	120.9	44½	139.8	50½	158.65	56½	177.5	62½	196.35
39	122.52	45	141.37	51	160.23	57	179.	63	197.92
39½	124.1	45½	142.94	51½	161.79	57½	180.64	63½	199.49
40	125.66	46	144.52	52	163.36	58	182.21	64	201.
40½	127.23	46½	146.	52½	164.93	58½	183.78	64½	202.63
41	128.8	47	147.65	53	166.5	59	185.35	65	204.2

EXAMPLE.

Required the circumference of a circle of 7 inches diameter. See the above Table; in column 1st, is 7 inches diameter, and against that, in column 2d, is 21.99, or what might be considered 22.

The following Rules, taken from the "Engineer's Text Book," are inserted for the convenience of the practical carpenter.

TO FIND THE AREA OF A CIRCLE.

Rule 1.—Multiply half the circumference by half the diameter, and the product will be the area.

Rule 2.—Square the diameter, and multiply that square by the decimal .7854 for the area.

Rule 3.—Square the circumference, and multiply that square by the decimal .07958.

TO FIND THE WEIGHT OF LEAD.

Rule.—Find by calculation the number of cubic inches in the piece, and multiply the sum by .41015, and the product will be the weight in lbs.

TO FIND THE WEIGHT OF BRASS.

Rule.—Find the number of cubic inches in the piece. Multiply by .3112, and the product will be the weight in pounds.

TO FIND THE WEIGHT OF WROUGHT IRON.

Rule.—Find the number of cubic inches in the piece, and multiply by the weight of 1 cubic inch, which is .2816, and the product is the weight in pounds.

TO FIND THE WEIGHT OF CAST IRON.

The multiplier is .2607, weight of a cubic inch.

SPECIFICATIONS

Of materials and labor suitable for the erection of the Italian Villa, Design I.

The specifications given below may be adapted, with some alterations, to almost any building of the same character. The Villa for which these specifications were originally drawn, was designed for William M. Bickford, Esq., of Worcester, Mass., which he is now erecting, and is similar to Design I. It cannot be expected that we should publish all the details for such a dwelling; hence, the references made to plans not found in this work.

SIZE OF HOUSE.

The house is to be of such dimensions as to admit of the rooms being finished as large as they are represented on the plans.

CELLAR.

The cellar to extend under the whole house, and to be eight feet from the bottom to the top of the underpinning. The wall, two feet six inches thick at the bottom and one foot eight inches at the top, to be made of large block stone well laid, and to be pointed with good lime mortar; to be carried up with a good face to the bottom of the underpinning with stone, and thence, on the inside of the underpinning, up to the sills, with brick-work. In those places where the underpinning sets out from the sills, under the porches or porticos, the wall is to be carried up to the sills, in place of the underpinning, with eight inch brick-work. The cellar to be divided, as per plan, with a brick wall eight inches thick, commencing at the bottom with *hard burnt* brick;—to be brick piers twelve inches square, to support the sills, where they are marked on the plan;—to have a drain, not less than eight inches square, well stoned and covered; also, doors in the partition walls, to afford a passage from one apartment to another, and a door from without, having good curb-stones and stone steps; the drain and doors to be located in such places as the owner may direct.

UNDERPINNING.

The underpinning to be two feet eight inches in height, and of fine hammered stone, well set, with the upper edge straightened and ends squared; the ends next to the cellar windows quoined. That part of the underpinning under the porticos to be of the same height as the other, and to rest on a dwarf wall commencing three feet below the surface of the ground. The front steps and buttresses to be of the same kind of stone and finish as the underpinning.

FRAMING.

The sills to be of the best chestnut timber, and the rest of the frame of the best northern hard pine, free from large knots and shakes. The floor joists jointed crowning, and the posts, studs, and girts jointed straight on their outer edges; the whole frame to be braced in every part where it is necessary.

The floor timbers in the *back part* may be one inch less in depth than in *front.*

The sizes of the timbers suitable for this house are given below:

	Inches.
Outside sills,	8×8
Cross sills,	9×8
First floor joists,	10×2½
Posts, main part,	8×6
Posts, back part,	7×5
Studs, main part,	6×2
Girts, main part,	8×6
Studs, back part,	5×2
Girts, back part,	7×5
Second floor joists,	9×2½
Plates, all around,	7×6
Third floor joists,	8×2
Beams, or Upper Girts,	8×6
Rafters, main part,	7×3
Rafters, back part,	6×3
Furring, on the ceiling,	3×1
Partition, first story,	4×2
Partition, second story,	3×2
Partition, back part,	3×2
Braces,	4×5

COVERING.

The outside to be well boarded with planed unmatched boards, of soft or white pine, thoroughly nailed, and sheathed with good eastern boards, well seasoned, well nailed, and smoothed to a *straight edge;*—the sheathing boards not to exceed five inches in width,—the joints matched and well painted with white lead and linseed oil; the corners at the angles of the house mitred together. For the finishing of sheathing around the windows, and for making the cornice, battlement, bracket, frieze, and gutters, see plan.

ROOFS.

The roofs, including those of the porticos, to be *first* covered with square-edged boards, about six inches wide, planed to an even thickness, the joints being left open about one eighth of an inch, and *then* with *tin* of the best quality and workmanship; the tinning to be continued through the gutters, to the edge of the cornice. The chimneys to be properly leaded, and every other place about the roofs where it is necessary.

FLOORS.

The under floors to be made of good northern pine boards, planed, matched, and well nailed; the upper floors of good floor boards free from large knots and shakes, and not to exceed eight inches in width, well nailed, and *cut in against the mop-boards.* The floor in the kitchen to be made of Georgia pine, well oiled and varnished; those in the drawing-room and parlor, traversed and made perfectly straight and level.

PARTITIONS.

The partitions to be made of good stock, jointed to such width as is given in the table, set *edgewise,* and bridged in two places. Those partitions around the closets and rooms of minor importance, may be set *flatwise.* All the partition joists, and all the furrings, set one foot from centre to centre.

The house to be divided into rooms throughout, as shown on the plan.

WINDOWS.

In first story, main part, each window, twelve lights, 24 by 14; in second story, each window, twelve lights, 20 by 14, excepting the one over the balcony in front, of fifteen lights, nine in the lower casement. In first story, *back* part, lights 16 by 12; in second story, lights 15 by 12.

All the sashes to be made of pine, one and seven eighths inches thick, and double hung with pulleys, weights, cords, &c., of the best quality.

The glass, in front windows, to be French plate; all the other, Redford crown glass, except that in back part, which is to be second quality of Redford, or Saranac.

PLASTERING.

The first and second stories of main part to be lathed and plastered with two coats of brown mortar, made perfectly even, and hard finished. The first and second stories of *back* part to be lathed and plastered with two coats, and the ceilings hard finished. The parlor, drawing-room, dining-room, vestibule, and entry, to have a small cornice; also, centre-pieces; one in the parlor, two in the drawing-room, one in the dining-room, one in the vestibule, and one in the entry. The bath-room and conservatory sheathed all around with planed and matched boards.

CHIMNEYS.

The chimneys, commencing at the bottom of the cellar with *hard-burnt* brick, to be carried up and *topped out*, as shown on the plan, with *pressed* brick;—to be as many fire-places as the owner may require, each having a separate flue extending to the top of the chimney.

The parlor, drawing and dining rooms, each to have marble chimney-pieces and hearths; the other hearths to be of pressed brick. The kitchen chimney to be fitted for a cooking-range, and a copper boiler, with an iron door, which will hold not less than thirty gallons; and to have a good-sized oven with a cast-iron door; to be an ash-pit formed in the basement of the chimney, having two cast-iron doors, one above and the other below.

HEIGHT OF STORIES.

The first story of main part to finish thirteen feet; the second story, twelve feet.

The first story of *back* part to finish eleven feet; the second story, ten feet. The attics unfinished, and without floors. Cupola as per plan.

PORTICOS.

The porticos in front to be made as per plan and elevation; see, also, details. The floors to be made of Georgia pine, one inch and a half thick, and four inches wide, with openings of one eighth of an inch; the timbers or bearings placed not more than eight inches apart. The underpinning to be on a level with that of the house. (See elevation and plan.) The *whole* front edge of the floors of the porticos to be about six inches thick; the roofs, like those on the house, to have small tin gutters in the top of the cornice. The columns, cornice, and all the other finish, as per plan.

FOLDING SHUTTERS.

The parlor and drawing-room to have folding shutters on the inside of the windows, divided into four parts vertically, and three horizontally. The shutters made of the best Eastern stock, well seasoned, and well hung, with trimmings and fastenings to correspond with the doors.

CHINA CLOSET.

China closet, located as per plan, with drawers on two sides, and with shelves, cupboards, and doors to suit the proprietor. Store-room fitted up with cupboard and shelves.

DOORS.

Doors in first story, main part, 7 feet 3 inches by 3 feet 3 inches, and 1 3-4 inches thick. In second story, doors 7 feet by 3, of the same thickness as the former. In first story, *back* part, doors 6 feet 10 inches by 2 feet 10 inches; in second story, 6 feet 8 inches by 2 feet 8 inches, and 1 1-2 inches thick in each story. Outside doors, 1 7-8 inches in thickness. For the form, see plan.

Here let the student or builder specify the quality of the doors, trimmings, &c.

STAIRS.

Front stairs, located as per plan, with mahogany railing and scroll; the railing and stairs to continue to the cupola, made of the best stock and workmanship.

DOOR AND WINDOW FINISH.

Finish for doors, windows, &c., in the parlor, drawing-room, and hall, both above and below, to be the same as represented on the plan. To be the same kind of finish, with the exception of the cornice, and some slight variations in size, in all the other rooms of main part. In the *back* part, a plain finish with a band moulding is all that is necessary.

BLINDS.

Blinds to all the windows in the house, well hung, and secured by proper fastenings; the lower part of each blind to have movable shades or slats. Painted with four coats, the last two of Paris green.

PAINTING.

All the exterior of the building to have three good coats of German white lead and best linseed oil, put on at proper times. The *interior*, excepting the floors, to have the same number of coats, of the same quality, neatly put on.

SINK AND FIXTURES.

Sink to be located, as shown on the plan, with two good copper pumps, one for soft, and the other for hard water, connected with two pipes, leading, one to the well of 1 3-4 inches calibre, and the other to the cistern of 1 1-2 inches calibre. The pipe that leads to the well to be tinned on the inner surface the whole length, and as far on the *outer* surface as it hangs in the water in the well. The cistern to be composed of brick and cement, and situated in the back cellar ; to be good pipes attached to the conductors to carry the water to the cistern, and a pipe of a calibre not less than 1 1-2 inches, to convey the water from the sink to the drain.

WATER WORKS.

A cistern, situated in the bath-room, six feet six inches from the floor, to be sufficiently large to contain five hundred gallons, and made of two thicknesses of plank, with a space of four inches between them, the space to be filled with tan, or any other substance that will prevent the water from freezing in the cistern. The spaces between the studs of the exterior walls of the bath-room filled with brick-work ;—the ceiling covered with moss or hair to the depth of eight or ten inches, and overlaid with boards.

The cistern to be supplied with water by a force-pump in the wash-room near the boiler, and a pipe 1 1-2 inches in diameter, so constructed as to draw the water from the cistern in the cellar and force it, as also water from the boiler, to the bathing-tub, as well as to the cistern in the bath-room. Also, a small sink in the bath-room, with a pipe and faucet for the purpose of drawing water from the upper cistern. The pipe-box, placed perpendicularly in the partition, reaching from the upper cistern to the cellar, should be large enough to permit all the pipes to pass, viz., the receiving pipe, discharging pipe, and a large pipe connected with the cistern above, the last not less than two inches in diameter, extending to the cellar, then dividing into branches three fourths of an inch in diameter, carried along in the cellar under the chambers, then up in the partitions to sinks prepared for the purpose, which may be in the form of furniture ; each sink to have a small discharging pipe.

A CATALOGUE

OF THE PRINCIPAL STYLES OF ANCIENT TEMPLES, ARRANGED UNDER ONE HEAD, FOR THE CONVENIENCE OF THE STUDENT.

AMPHIPROSTYLE. — A term applied to a temple having a portico or porch in the rear as well as in the front, but without columns at the sides. This species of temple never exceeded the use of four columns in the front and four in the rear. It differed from the temple in *antis*, in having columns instead of antæ at the angles in the portico.

ARÆOSTYLE. — One of the five proportions used by the ancients for regulating the intercolumniations or intervals between the columns in porticos and colonnades.

ARÆOSYSTYLE. — A term used by the French architects to denote the method of proportioning the intervals between columns coupled or ranged in pairs, as invented by Perrault, and introduced in the principal façade of the Louvre.

DIASTYLE. — That distance between columns which consists of three diameters, or, according to some, of four diameters. The term is sometimes used adjectively, to signify that the building is arranged with those intervals between the columns.

DIPTERAL. — In ancient architecture, a temple having a double range of columns on each of its flanks.

EUSTYLE. — See COLONNADE.

HYPAETHRAL. — A building or temple without a roof. The temples of this class are arranged by Vitruvius under the seventh order, which had ten columns on each front, and surrounded by a double portico as in dipteral temples. The cell was without roof, whence the name, but it generally had round it a portico of two ranges of columns, one above the other.

MONOTRIGLYPH. — A term applied to an intercolumniation in which only one triglyph and two metopæ are introduced.

PERIPTERAL. — A temple surrounded by a periptery, that is, encompassed by columns.

PERISTYLE. — See COLONNADE.

PROSTYLE. — A portico in which the columns stand in advance of the building to which they belong.

PSEUDODIPTERAL, or FALSE DIPTERAL. — A disposition of antiquity wherein there were eight columns in front and only one range round the cell. It is called false or imperfect, because the cell only occupying the width of four columns, the sides from the columns to the walls of the cell have no columns therein, though the front and rear present a column in the middle of the void.

PYCNOSTYLE. — See COLONNADE.

SYSTYLE. — See COLONNADE.

A GLOSSARY

OF

ARCHITECTURAL TERMS.

FROM GWILT'S ENCYCLOPÆDIA

A.

ABACUS. — The upper member of the capital of a column, and serving as a crowning, both to the capital and to the whole column. In the Tuscan, Doric, and ancient Ionic orders, it is a flat, square member.

ABBEY. — Properly, the building adjoining to or near a convent or monastery, for the residence of the head of the house, — Abbot or Abbess. It is often used for the church attached to the establishment, as, also, for the buildings composing the whole establishment. In such establishments, the church was usually grand, and splendidly decorated.

ACANTHUS. — A spiny, herbaceous plant, found in various parts of the Levant. Its leaf is said by Vitruvius to have been the model on which the Grecian architects formed the leaves of the Corinthian capital.

ACROPOLIS. — The upper town or citadel of a Grecian city, usually the site of the original settlement, and chosen by the colonists for its natural strength.

ACUTE ANGLE. — A term used in geometry to denote an angle less than 90°, that is, less than a right angle.

AISLE. — A term chiefly used by the English architect to signify the side subdivisions in a church, usually separated from the nave or centre division by pillars or columns; but, in more modern times, this term is used to denote the alley, or passage between the pews or slips.

ALLEY. — An aisle, or any part of a church left open for access to another part. In towns, a passage narrower than a lane. A walk in a garden.

ALMONRY. — Properly, a closet or repository for the reception of broken victuals set apart as alms for the poor; but more generally used to denote a house near the church, in abbeys or their gates, provided with various offices for distributing the alms of the convent, and for the dwelling of the almoner.

ALTAR. — A sort of pedestal whereon sacrifices were anciently offered to some deity. In modern churches, the communion tables, and, figuratively, a church; a place of worship.

ALTO RILIEVO. — See *Rilievo*.

AMBULATORY. — A sheltered place for exercise in walking; a cloister; a gallery.

AMPHITHEATRE. — An edifice formed by the junction of two theatres at the proscenium, so as to have seats all round the periphery, — a contrivance by which all the spectators, being ranged about on seats rising the one above the other, saw equally well what passed on the arena or space enclosed by the lowest range of seats.

ANGLE. — The mutual inclination of two lines meeting in a point, called indifferently the angular point, vertex, or point of concourse; the two lines are called legs.

ANGLE BRACKET. — A bracket placed in the vertex of an angle, and not at right angles with the sides.

ANGLE CAPITAL. — In ancient Greek architecture, the Ionic capitals used to the flank columns which have one of their volutes placed at an angle of 135° with the planes of the front and returning frieze. This term is also applied to the modern Ionic capital, in which the whole of the four volutes have an angular direction.

ANGLE OF VISION. — The angle under which an object or objects are seen, and upon which their apparent magnitudes depend. In practical perspective it should not exceed sixty degrees.

ANNULET. — A small fillet whose horizontal section is circular. The neck or under side of the Doric capital is decorated with these thin fillets, listels, or bands, whose number varies in different examples.

ANTA, (plural Antæ.) — The joints or square posts supporting the lintels of doors. There are three kinds of antæ; those of porches or jamb ornaments; angular antæ, being such as show two faces on the walls of a temple; and those on the longitudinal walls of its cell.

ANTE-CHAMBER, or ANTE-ROOM. — An apartment through which access is obtained to another chamber or room. One in which servants wait, and strangers are detained till the person to be spoken with is at leisure.

APERTURE. — An opening through any body. In a wall it has usually three straight sides, two whereof are perpendicular to the horizon, and the third parallel to it, connecting the lower ends of the vertical sides. The materials forming the vertical sides are called *jambs*, and the lower level side is called the *sill*, and the upper part the *head*. This last is either a curved or flat arch. Apertures are made for entrance, light, or ornament.

APIARY. — A place for keeping beehives. Sometimes, this is a small house with openings for bees in front, and a door behind, which is kept locked for security. Sometimes, it is an area wherein each particular beehive is chained down to a post and padlocked.

AQUEDUCT. — A conduit or channel for conveying water from one place to another; but more particularly applied to structures for the purpose of conveying the water of distant springs across valleys, for the supply of large cities.

ARABESQUE. — A building after the Arabian style. The term is more commonly used to denote that sort of ornament which adorns the walls, pavements, and ceilings of Arabian and Saracenic buildings.

ARC. — In geometry, a portion of a circle or other curve line. The arc of a circle is the measure of the angle formed by two straight lines drawn from its extremities to the centre of the circle.

ARCADE. — A series of apertures or recesses with arched ceilings or sofites.

ARCH. — A mechanical arrangement of blocks of any hard material disposed in the line of some curve, and supporting one another by their mutual pressure. The solid extremities on or against which the arch rests are called the *abutments.*

ARCHITRAVE. — The lower of the three principal members of the entablature of an order, being, as its name imports, the chief beam employed in it, and resting immediately on the columns.

ARCHITRAVE CORNICE. — An entablature consisting of an architrave and cornice only, without the interposition of a frieze. It is never used with columns or pilasters, unless through want of weight.

ARCHIVOLT. — The ornamental band of moulding round the arch-stones of an arch, which terminates horizontally upon the impost. It is decorated, as to the members, analagously with the architrave, which, in arcades, it may be said to represent. It differs in the different orders.

AREA. — In architecture, a small court or place, often sunk below the general surface of the ground, before windows in the basement story. It is also used to denote a small court, level with the ground. In geometry, the superficial content of any figure.

ARENA. — The central space in a Roman amphitheatre, wherein the gladiators fought.

ARSENAL. — A public establishment for the deposition of arms and warlike stores.

ARTIFICER. — A person who works with his hands in the manufacture of anything; an artist; a mechanic.

ASHLAR, or ASHLER. — Common or free stones, as brought from the quarry, of different lengths and thicknesses.

ASTRAGAL. — A small moulding of a semi-circular profile.

ATTIC, or ATTIC ORDER. — A low order of architecture, commonly used over a principal order, never with columns, but usually, with antæ or small pilasters.

ATTIC BASE. — The base of a column consisting of an upper and lower torus, a scotia and fillets between them.

AVIARY. — A house or apartment set apart for keeping and breeding birds.

AWNING. — Any covering intended as a screen from the sun, or protection from the rain.

B.

BALCONY. — A projection from the external wall of a house, borne by columns, and usually placed before windows or openings, and protected on the extremity of the projection by a railing of balusters or iron-work.

BALUSTER. — A species of small column belonging to a balustrade. This term is also used to denote the lateral part of the volute of the Ionic capital.

BALUSTRADE. — A parapet or protecting fence formed of balusters, sometimes employed for real use, and sometimes merely for ornament.

BAND. — A flat member or moulding, smaller than a facia. The word, however, is applied to narrow members somewhat wider than fillets; and the word facia.

BANISTER. — A vulgar term for baluster.

BARGE BOARDS. — The inclined projecting boards placed at the gable of a building, and hiding the horizontal timbers of a roof.

BASEMENT. — The lower story of a building, whether above or below the ground.

BASE. — In geometry, the lower part of a figure or body. The *base of a solid* is the surface on which it rests.

BASSO-RELIEVO. — See *Relievo.*

BATH. — An apartment or series of apartments for bathing.

BATTEN. — A scantling, or piece of stuff from two to six inches broad, and from five eighths of an inch to two inches thick.

BATTLEMENTS. — Indentations on the top of a wall, parapet, or other building.

BATTER. — A term used by artificers to signify that a body does not stand upright, but inclines from a person standing before it. When, on the contrary, it inclines towards a person, it is said to overhang.

BAY WINDOW. — A window placed in the bay or bow of a window; called also an oriel window.

BELFRY. — The upper part of the steeple of a church, for the reception of the bells. It is sometimes used more especially in respect of the timber framing by which the bells are supported.

BELVEDERE. — A turret or lantern raised for the enjoyment of a prospect: also, a small edifice in gardens.

BLANK WINDOW. — One which has the appearance of a real window, but is merely formed in the recess of the wall.

BLANK DOOR. — A door either shut to prevent a passage, or one placed in the back of a recess, where there is no entrance, having the appearance of a real door.

BRACKET. — A supporting piece for a shelf. It is sometimes used in stairs and in eave cornices.

BUILDER. — A person who contracts for performing the different artificers' works in a building.

BUILDING. — Used as a substantive, is the mass of materials shaped into an edifice. As a participle it is the constructing and raising an edifice suited to the purposes for which it is erected.

BUNDLE PILLAR. — In Gothic architecture, a column consisting of a number of small pillars round its circumference.

BUTMENT. — The same as abutment. The solid part of a pier from which the arch immediately springs. Butments are artificial or natural. The former are usually formed of masonry or brick-work, and the latter are the rock or other solid materials on the banks of the river in the case of a bridge, which receives the foot on the arch.

BUTTERY. — A store-room for provisions, which, if possible, should be on the north side of a building.

C.

CABIN. — A term applied to the huts and cottages of poor people, and to those of persons in a savage state of life.

Cabinet. — A retired room in an edifice, set apart for writing, study, or the preservation of anything curious or valuable.

Caliber. — The greatest extent or diameter of a round body.

Campanile. — A tower for the reception of bells, usually, in Italy, separated from the church.

Canal. — A duct for the conveyance of a fluid; thus, the canal of an aqueduct is the part through which the water flows.

Canopy. — An ornamented covering over a seat of state; and, in its extended signification, any covering which affords protection from above. It is also the label or projecting roof that surrounds the arches and heads of Gothic niches.

Capital. — The head or uppermost member of any part of a building, but generally applied, in a restricted sense, to that of a column or pilaster of the several orders.

Carpenter. — An artificer who cuts, forms, and shapes timbers for the purposes of giving strength and support to the various parts which are of timber in the construction of buildings.

Carpentry. — An assemblage of pieces of timber connected by framing, or letting them into each other, as are the pieces of a roof, floor, centre, &c. It is distinguished from a joinery by being put together without the use any other edge tools than the axe, adze, saw, and chisel; whereas, joinery requires the use of the plane.

Caryatides. — Figures used instead of columns for the support of an entablature.

Casement. — A glazed frame or sash, opening on hinges affixed to the vertical sides of the frame into which it is fitted.

Castle. — A building fortified for military defence; also, a house with towers, usually encompassed with walls, and moats, and having a dungeon or keep in the centre.

Catacombs. — Subterraneous places for burying the dead.

Cathedral. — The principal church of a province or diocese, where the throne of archbishop or bishop is placed.

Cavetto. — A hollowed moulding, whose profile is the quadrant of a circle. It is principally used in cornices.

Ceiling. — The upper horizontal or curved surface of an apartment, opposite the floor; usually finished with plastered work.

Cell. — In ancient architecture, the part of a temple within the walls. It was also called the *naos*, whence our *nave* in a church.

Cesspool. — A well sunk under the mouth of a drain, to receive the sediment which might choke up its passage.

Chamber. — Properly, a room vaulted or arched; but the word is now generally used in a more restricted sense, to signify an apartment appropriated to lodging.

Chamfer. — The arris of anything originally right angled, cut aslope or bevel, so that the plane it then forms is inclined less than a right angle to the other planes with which it intersects.

Chancel. — That part of the eastern end of a church in which the altar is placed.

Chapel. — A building for religious worship, erected separately from a church, and served by a chaplain.

Chimney Piece. — An ornamental decoration applied to the aperture of a chimney opening.

Choir. — The part of a church in which the choristers sing divine service.

Church. — A building dedicated to the performance of Christian worship.

Cincture. — The ring, list, or fillet at the top and bottom of a column, which divides the shaft of the column from its capital and base.

Cinquefoil. — An ornament used in the pointed style of architecture. It consists of five curved pendants inscribed in a pointed arch, or in a circular ring, applied to windows and panels.

Cistern. — A reservoir for water, whether sunk below or formed of planks of wood above ground.

Coffer. — A sunk panel in vaults and domes, and also, in the soffite or under side of the Corinthian and Composite cornices, and usually decorated in the centre with a flower. But the application of the term is general to any sunk plank in a ceiling or soffite.

Colonnade. — A range of columns. If the columns are four in number, it is called *tetrastyle;* if six in number, *hexastyle;* when there are eight, *octo style;* when ten, *decastyle;* and so on, according to the Greek numerals. When a colonnade is in front of a building, it is called a *portico;* when surrounding a building, a *peristyle;* and when double or more, *polystyle.* The colonnade is, moreover, designated according to the nature of the intercolumniations introduced, as follows: — *pycrostyle,* when the space between the columns is one diameter and a half of a column; *systyle,* when it is of two diameters; *eustyle,* when of two diameters and a quarter; *diastyle* when three, and *arœostyle* when four.

Composite Order. — This order, as its name imports, is a compound of other orders, — the Corinthian and Ionic, — and was received into the regular number of orders by Vitruvius.

Conservatory. — A building for preserving curious and rare exotic plants.

Contour. — The external lines which bound and terminate a figure.

Coping. — The highest and covering course of masonry or brick-work in a wall.

Corbeil. — A carved basket, with sculptured flowers and fruit, used as the finishing of some ornament. This is also applied to the bell of the Corinthian capital.

Corinthian Order. — See

Cornice. — Any moulded projection which crowns or finishes the part to which it is affixed.

Corona. — A member of the cornice, with a broad, vertical face, and usually of considerable projection.

Court. — An uncovered area before or behind the house, or in the centre of it, in which latter case it is often surrounded by buildings on its four sides.

Cove. — Any kind of concave moulding or vault; but the term, in its usual acceptation, is the quadrantal profile between the ceiling of a room and its cornice.

Cramp. — An iron instrument, about four feet long, having a screw at one end, and a movable shoulder at the other, employed by carpenters and joiners for forcing mortice and tenon work together.

Crescent. — A building, or rather a series of buildings, which on the plan is disposed in the arc of a circle.

Crocket. — One of the small ornaments usually placed on the angles of pinnacles, pediments, canopies, &c., in Gothic architecture, and most commonly disposed at equal distances from each other.

Cupola. — A term, properly speaking, which is confined to the *under-side*, or ceiling part of a dome.

Curbstones. — Those in the foot-paving of a street which divide it from the carriage-paving, above which they are, or ought to be, raised.

Curtail Step. — The first or bottom step by which stairs are ascended, ending at the furthest point from the wall, in which it is placed in a scroll; perhaps taking its name from the step curling round like a cur's tail.

Custom House. — An edifice erected for the receipt of the customs' duties, payable on the importation and exportation of merchandise.

Cyma. — A moulding taking its name from its contour, resembling that of a wave, being hollow in its upper part, and swelling below. Of this moulding there are two sorts, the cyma recta, and the cyma reversa. By the workmen these are called *ogees*.

Cymatium. — The upper moulding of a cornice.

D.

Dado. — The die, or part in the middle of the pedestal of a column, between the base and cornice. It is of a cubic form, whence the name of die.

Dentils. — The small, square blocks or projections in the bed-mouldings of cornices in the Ionic, Corinthian, Composite, and, occasionally, Doric orders. Their breadth should be half their height.

Details. — A term usually applied to the drawings on a larger scale, for the use of builders, and generally called *working-drawings*.

Diameter. — A straight line passing through the centre of a geometrical figure, as that of a circle, ellipse, or hyperbola.

Dog-legged Stairs. — Such as are solid between the upper flight, or such as have no well-hole, and in which the rail and balusters of both progressive and retrogressive flight fall in the same vertical plane.

Dome. — The spherical, or other figure, convex roof over a circular or polygonal building.

Doric Order.

Dormer. — A window placed on the inclined plane of the roof of a house, the frame being placed vertically on the rafters.

Dormitory. — A large sleeping-room, capable of containing many beds.

Draught. — The representation of a building on paper, explanatory of the various parts of the interior and exterior, by means of plans, elevations, and sections, drawn to a scale, by which all the parts are exhibited in the same proportion as the parts of the edifice intended to be represented.

Drip. — See *Corona.*

Drops. — The frusta of cones in the Doric order, used under the triglyphs in the architrave.

E.

Eaves. — The lowest edges of the inclined sides of a roof, which project beyond the face of the walls.

Echinus. — The same as the *ovola*, or *quarter round*, though the moulding is only properly so called when carved with eggs and anchors.

Edifice. — A word synonymous with fabric, building, erection. The word is, however, more commonly employed to denote architectural erections distinguished for grandeur, dignity, and importance.

19

Egyptian Architecture. — See

Elevation. — A geometrical projection drawn on a plane perpendicular to the horizon.

Ellipse, or Ellipsis. — One of the conic sections produced by cutting a cone entirely through the curved surface, neither parallel to the base, nor making a sub-contrary section; so that the ellipsis, like the circle, is a curve that returns into itself, and completely encloses a space.

Entablature. — The whole of the parts of an order above a column. The assemblage is divided into three parts; viz., architecture, frieze, and cornice.

F.

Fabric. — A general term applied to a large and important building.

Façade. — The face or front of any building towards a street, court, garden, or other place. A term, however, more commonly used to signify the principal front.

Facia, or Fascia. — A flat member of an order or of a building, like a flat band or broad fillet.

Festoon. — A sculptured representation of flowers, drapery, and foliage, looped or suspended at intervals on the walls.

Figure. — In a general sense, the terminating extremes or surface of a body. In geometry, any plane surface comprehended within a certain line or lines.

Fillet. — A narrow, flat band, listel, or annulet, used for the separation of one moulding from another, and to give breadth and firmness to the upper edge of a crowning moulding, as in a cornice.

Fixture. — A term applied to all articles of a personal nature affixed to land. This annexation must be by the article being let into, or united with, the land, or with some substance previously connected therewith.

Flank. — That part of a return body which joins the front.

Floated Lath and Plaster. — Plastering of three coats, whereof the first is *pricking-up*, the second floating, or floated work, and the last of fine stuff.

Floated Work. — Plastering rendered perfectly plane by means of a *float*.

Forum. — In ancient architecture, a public market; also, a place where the common courts were held, and law pleadings carried on. Fora of the Romans were large, open squares, surrounded by porticos, parts whereof answered for market places, other parts for public meetings of the inhabitants, and other parts for courts of justice; the forum was also occasionally used for shows of gladiators.

Freeze. — See *Frieze.*

Fresco Painting. — A method of painting by incorporating colors with plaster before it is dry, by which it becomes as permanent as the wall itself.

Frette, or Fret. — A species of ornament consisting of one or more small fillets, meeting in vertical and horizontal directions.

Frieze. — That member in the entablature of an order, between the architrave and cornice.

Furring. — The fixing of thin scantlings or laths upon the edges of any number of timbers in a range, when such timbers are out of the surface they were intended to form, either from their gravity, or in consequence of an original deficiency of the timbers in their depth.

G.

Gallery. — An apartment of a house, for different purposes. A common passage to several rooms in any upper story is called a gallery.
Geometry. — That science which treats of the objects of figured space.
Glyph. — A sunken channel, the term being usually employed in reference to a vertical one.
Groin. — The line formed by the intersection of two arches which cross each other at any angle.
Ground. — The plan of the story of a house level with the surface of the ground, or a few steps above it.
Guttæ. — See *Drops*.

H.

Hand-Rail of a Stair. — A rail raised upon slender posts, called balusters, to prevent persons falling down the well-hole, as also to assist them in ascending and descending.
Hecatompedon. — A temple of a hundred feet in length.
Hexagon. — In geometry, a plain figure bounded by six straight lines, which, when equal, constitute the figure a regular hexagon.
Horizontal Cornice. — The level part of the cornice of a pediment under the two inclined cornices.
Hospital. — A building for the reception of the sick poor, for insane persons, and, sometimes, for particular diseases.
Hot House. — A general term for the glass buildings used in gardening, and including stoves, greenhouses, and conservatories.
House. — A human habitation, or place of abode of a family.
Hung, (Double and Single.) — A term applied to sashes; the first, when both the upper and lower sash are balanced by weights, for raising and depressing; and the last, when only one, usually the lower one, is balanced over the pulleys.

I.

Ice House. — A subterranean depot for preserving ice during the winter.
Imperial. — A species of dome, whose profile is pointed towards the top, and widens towards the base, thus forming a curve of contrary flexure.
Impost. — The capital of a pier or pilaster which receives an arch.
Inclined Plane. — One of the five simple mechanical powers, whose theory is deduced from the decomposition of forces.
Intercolumniation. — The distance between two columns, measured at the lower part of their shafts.
Ionic Order. — See

J.

Jambs. — The sides of an aperture which connect the two sides of a wall.
Joiner. — The artisan who joins wood by glue, framing, or nails, for the finishings of a building.
Joinery. — The practice of framing or joining wood for the internal finishings of houses.

K.

Kitchen. — The apartment or office of a house wherein the operations of cookery are carried on.

L.

Label. — In Gothic architecture, the drip or hood-moulding over an aperture when it is returned square.
Labyrinth Fret. — A fret with many turnings, in the form of a labyrinth.
Lewis, or **Lewisson.** — An instrument said to have been used in England by the builders of the middle ages, to raise stones of more than ordinary weight to the upper part of a building.
Lintel. — A horizontal piece of timber or stone over a door, window, or other opening, to discharge the superincumbent weight.
List, or **Listel.** — The same as fillet.
Lobby. — An enclosed space surrounding or communicating with one or more apartments.
Lock. — A well-known instrument, consisting of springs and bolts, for fastening doors, drawers, chests, &c.
Luthern. — The same as *Dormer*.

M.

Mansion. — A large house; a term more usually applied to one in the country.
Member. — Any part of an edifice, or any moulding in a collection of mouldings, as of those in a cornice, capital, base, &c.
Metopa. — The square space in the frieze between the triglyphs of the Doric order.
Minster. — A church to which an ecclesiastical fraternity has been or is attached. The name is occasionally applied to cathedrals.
Minute. — A term given to the sixtieth part of the lower diameter of a column, being a subdivision used for measuring the minuter parts of an order.
Miter, or **Mitre.** — See *Bevel*.
Modillian. — A projection under the corona of the richer orders, resembling a bracket.
Moresque Architecture. — The style of building peculiar to the Moors and Arabs.
Mosaic. — A mode of representing objects by the inlaying of small cubes of glass, stone, marble, shells, wood, &c.
Mosque. — A Mohammedan temple or place of worship.
Mouldings. — The ornamental contours or forms applied to the edges of the projecting or receding members of an order.
Mullion, or **Munnion.** — In pointed architecture, the vertical post or bar which divides a window into several lights.
Mutule. — A projecting ornament of the Doric cornice, which occupies the place of the modillion in the other order, and supposed to represent the end rafters.

N.

Nave. — The body of a church, or place where the people are seated, reaching from the rail or partition of the choir to the principal entrance.
Neck of a Capital. — The space in the Doric order between the astragal on the shaft and the annulet of the capital.
Newel. — The upright cylinder or pillar round which, in a winding staircase, the steps turn, and are supported from the bottom to the top.
Niche. — A cavity or hollow place in the thickness of a wall, for the reception of a statue, vase, &c.
Notch-board. — A board which is grooved or notched for the reception and support of the ends of steps in a staircase.

O.

Ogee. — A moulding, the same as the *Cyma reversa.*

Orchestra. — The enclosed part of a music-room, wherein the instrumental and vocal performers are seated.

Order. — An assemblage of parts, consisting of a base, shaft, capital, architrave, frieze, and cornice.

Oriel, or Oriel Window. — A large bay or recessed window in a hall, chapel, or other apartment. It ordinarily projects from the outer face of the wall either in a semi-octagonal or diagonal plane, and is of varied kinds and sizes.

Oval. — A geometrical figure, whose boundary is a curve line returning into itself; it includes the ellipsis or mathematical oval, and all figures resembling it, though with different properties.

Ovolo. — A convex moulding, whose lower extremity recedes from a perpendicular line drawn from the upper extremity.

P.

Palace. — In England, a name given to the dwelling of a king or queen, a prince, and a bishop.

Panel. — A board whose edges are inserted into the groove of a thicker surrounding frame.

Parapet. — A small wall of any material for projection on the sides of bridges, quays, or high buildings.

Parlor. — A room for conversation, which, in the old monasteries, adjoined the buttery and pantry at the lower end of the hall. At the present day it is used to denote the room in a house where common visitors are received.

Pedestal. — The lowest division in an order of columns. It consists of three principal parts; the die or square trunk, the cornice or head, and the base or foot.

Pendent. — An ornament suspended from the summit of Gothic vaulting, very often elaborately decorated.

Perspective. — The science which teaches the art of representing objects on a definite surface, so as from a certain position to affect the eye in the same manner as the objects themselves would.

Piazza. — A square open space, surrounded by buildings. The term is very frequently, and very ignorantly, used to denote a walk under an arcade.

Piles. — Large timbers driven into the earth, upon whose heads is laid the foundation of a building in marshy and loose soils.

Pillar. — A column of irregular form, always disengaged, and always deviating from the proportions of the orders, whence the distinction between a column and a pillar.

Pinnacle. — A summit or apex. Its form is usually slender, and tapers to a point.

Plan. — The representation of the horizontal section of a building, showing its distribution, the form and extent of its various parts.

Plancer. — The same as the sofite or under surface of the corona; the word is, however, very often used generally to mean any sofite.

Plinth. — The lower square member of a base of a column or pedestal.

Pointing. — The raking out the mortar from between the joints of brick-work, and replacing the same with new mortar.

Porch. — An exterior appendage to a building, forming a covered approach to one of its principal doorways.

Portal. — The arch over a door or gate; the framework of a gate; the lesser gate, when there are two of different dimensions at one entrance.

Portico. — See *Colonnade.*

Post. — An upright piece of timber set in the earth.

Profile. — The vertical section of a body. It is principally used, in its architectural sense, to signify the contour of architectural members, as of bases, cornices, &c. The profile of an order is in fact the outline of the whole and its parts.

Projection. — The art of representing a body on a plane by drawing straight lines through a given point, or parallel from the contour and from the intermediate lines of the body.

Pulpit. — An elevated place, an enclosed stage or platform for a preacher in a church.

Purlins. — Horizontal pieces of timber, lying generally on the principal rafters of a roof to lessen the bearings of the common rafters.

Q.

Quarter Round. — The same as *Ovolo* and *Echinus*, being a moulding whose profile is the quadrant of a circle.

Quarterfoil. — A modern term denoting a form disposed in four segments of circles, and so called from its imagined resemblance to an expanded flower of four petals.

Quay. — A bank formed towards the sea, or on the side of a river, for free passage, or for the purpose of unloading merchandise.

Quirk. — A piece taken out of any ground-plot or floor; thus, if the ground-plan were square or oblong, and a piece were taken out of the corner, such piece is called a *quirk.*

Quirk-moulding. — One whose sharp and sudden return from its extreme projection to the rëentrant angle seems rather to partake of a straight line on the profile than of the curve.

Quoins. — A term applied to any external angle, but more especially applied to the angular courses of stone raised from the naked face of the wall, at the corner of a building, and called rustic quoins.

R.

Rabbet. — See *Rebate.*

Radius. — In geometry, the semi-diameter of a circle, or a right line drawn from the centre to the circumference.

Rafters. — The inclined timbers of a roof, whose edges are in the same plane which is parallel to the covering.

Rail. — A term applied in various ways, but more particularly to those pieces of timber or wood lying horizontally, whether between the panels of wainscoting or of doors, or under or over the compartments of balustrades, &c.

Raking. — A term applied to any member whose arrisses lie inclined to the horizon.

Reservoir. — An artificial pond, basin, or cistern, for the collection and supply of water.

Rilievo, or Relief. — The projecture from its ground of any architectural ornament.

Roof. — The exterior covering of a building.

Room. — An interior space or division of a house, separated from the remainder of it by walls or partitions, and entered by a door-way.

ROTUNDA, or ROTONDO. — A building circular on the interior and exterior, such as the Pantheon at Rome.

ROUGH-CAST. — A species of plastering used on external walls, consisting of a mixture of lime, small shells or pebbles, occasionally fragments of glass, and similar materials.

RUSTIC ORDER — A species of building wherein the faces of the stones are pricked with the point of a hammer.

RUSTIC WORK. — A mode of building masonry wherein the faces of the stones are left rough, the sides only being wrought smooth where the union of the stones takes place.

S.

SASH. — A frame for holding the glass of windows, and so formed as to be raised and depressed by means of pulleys.

SCANTLING. — The dimensions of a piece of timber in breadth and thickness.

SCOTIA. — The hollow moulding in the base of a column, between the fillets of the tori. It receives the name from being so much in the shadow.

SCROLL. — A convolved or spiral ornament, variously introduced.

SCULPTURE. — The art of imitating forms by chiselling and working away solid substances.

SHAFT. — The cylindrical part, or rather body, of a column, between the base and the capital.

SILL. — See *Cill* and *Aperture*.

SOFFITA, SOFFIT, or SOFITE. — A ceiling; the lower surface of a vault or arch. A term denoting the under horizontal face of the architrave between columns; the under surface of the corona of a cornice.

SPLAYED. — A term applied to whatever has one side making an oblique angle with the other.

STADIUM. — In ancient architecture, an open space wherein the athleti or wrestlers exercised running, and in which they contested the prizes. It signifies also the place itself where the public games were celebrated, often formed a part of the gymnasia. The word also denotes a measure of length, among the Grecians, of 125 paces.

STEEPLE. — A lofty erection attached to a church, chiefly intended to contain its bells.

STILE. — The vertical part of a piece of framing, into which, in joinery, the ends of the rails are fixed by mortises and tenons.

STORY. — One of the vertical divisions of a building; a series of apartments on the same level.

STUCCO. — A term indefinitely applied to calcareous cements of various descriptions.

STUFF. — A general term for the wood used by joiners.

SYMMETRY. — A system of proportion in a building, from which results from one part the measurement of all the rest.

T.

TÆNIA. — The fillet which separates the Doric frieze from the architrave.

TEMPLE. — Generally an edifice erected for the public exercise of religious worship.

TORUS. — A large moulding whose section is semi-circular, used in the bases of columns. The only difference between it and the astragal is in the size, the astragal being much smaller.

TRANSOM. — A beam across a window of two lights in height. If a window have no transom, it is called a clear story window.

TREFOIL. — In Gothic architecture, an ornament consisting of three cusps in a circle.

TRELLICE. — A reticulated framing made of thin bars of wood, for screens; windows where air is required for the apartment, &c.

TRIGLYPH. — The vertical tablets in the Doric frieze, chamfered on the two vertical edges, and having two channels in the middle, which are double channels to those at the angles.

TRUSS. — A combination of timber framing, so arranged, that, if suspended at two given points, and charged with one or more weights in certain others, no timber would press transversely upon any other except by timbers exerting equal and opposite forces.

TURRET. — A small tower, often crowning the angle of a wall, &c.

TYMPANUM. — The naked face of a pediment included between the level and raking mouldings.

U.

UNDERPINNING. — Bringing a wall up to the ground sill. The term is also used to denote the temporary support of a wall whose lower part or foundations are defective, and the bringing up new solid work whereon it is in future to rest.

V.

VANE. — A plate of metal, shaped like a banner, fixed on the summit of a tower or steeple, to show the direction of the wind.

VAULT. — An arched roof, over an apartment, concave towards the void, whose section may be that of any curve in the same direction.

VENETIAN DOOR. — A door having side-lights on each side for lighting an entrance hall.

VENETIAN WINDOW. — One formed with three apertures, separated by slender piers from each other, whereof the centre one is much larger than those on the sides.

VESTIBULE. — An apartment which serves as the medium of communication to another room or series of rooms.

VESTRY. — An apartment in, or attached to, a church, for the preservation of the sacred vestments and utensils.

VILLA. — A country-house for the residence of an opulent person.

VOLUTE. — A spiral scroll which forms the principal feature of the Ionic and Composite capitals.

W.

WELL-HOLE. — In a flight of stairs, the space left in the middle, beyond the ends of the steps.

www.ingramcontent.com/pod-product-compliance
Lightning Source LLC
LaVergne TN
LVHW010221110826
845151LV00004B/1166

* 9 7 8 1 4 2 5 5 2 6 5 1 1 *